MW00711907

STAG

A Bachelor's Last Night of Freedom

NIGHT

STAG NIGHT

A Bachelor's Last Night of Freedom

Edited by
CHRISTOPHER MEASOM

Designed by
TIMOTHY SHANER

welcome
BOOKS
New York • San Francisco

Published in 2009 by Welcome Books
An imprint of Welcome Enterprises, Inc.
6 West 18th Street, New York, NY 10011
Tel: 212-989-3200; Fax: 212-989-3205
www.welcomebooks.com

Publisher: Lena Tabori   Project Director: Alice Wong   Project Assistant: Robyn Curtis

Copyright © 2009 Night & Day Design LLC.
www.nightanddaydesign.biz
Additional copyright information on page 176.

1 3 5 7 9 10 8 6 4 2

All rights reserved. No part of this book may be reproduced or utilized in any form or
by any means, electronic or mechanical, including photocopying, recording, or by any
information storage or retrieval system, without permission in writing from the publisher.

Library of Congress Cataloging-in-Publication Data

Stag night : a bachelor's last night of freedom / edited by Christopher Measom ;
designed by Timothy Shaner.
    p. cm.
 ISBN 978-1-59962-063-3
 1. Bachelor parties--Planning. 2. Entertaining. 3. Group games. 4. Adult party
games. I. Measom, Christopher.
  GV1472.7.B33S84 2008
  793.2--dc22   2008033969

Printed in Singapore

CONTENTS

Games & Activities (cont.)

History of . . .

Stag Fare

Stagsploitation

Travel Ideas

Vintage Pulp & Other Tales

Hugh Hefner's *Playboy* magazine was originally called *Stag Party*, and it is that whole mid-20th-century bachelor aesthetic that inspired this book. Martinis, cigars, naughtish jokes, he-man pulp fiction—I've included all that—along with a dollop of 1950s-style angst from Paddy Chayefsky to add a bit of depth.

The art and stories are here to give a framework—sometimes a tongue-in-cheek one—to the heady days leading up to marriage, a truly overwhelming (not to mention seriously major) rite of passage. It seems that because the going has been known to get rough along this particular road, the bachelor party (full of jokes and smokes, camaraderie and letting loose) arose to help ease the way. And though the men of Hugh Hefner's day didn't invent this little get-together— nope, this party has been going on for at least 2500 years—they did have a certain groovy style.

But beyond this sometimes-comic, sometimes-nostalgic (sometimes-queasy) peek at stag night, this book is also meant to be a handy guide for the modern groom and his best man. For the groom it will help trigger ideas about how he wants to celebrate. And for the best man—whose awesome responsibility is organizing the fete—this book is an answer to his call for *help!* For it is he who has to round up and coordinate a whole lot of male energy—in all its devilish, adventurous, rough-and-tumble, loud, aggressive, goal-oriented, game-loving glory—and make a night of it. And, perhaps most important, he is responsible for making sure the groom comes through it all in one piece. (Rent the film *Mexican Sunrise* to see how things might go horribly awry.)

For a successful fiesta, the best man has to call on his creative, intuitive, nurturing, side—yes, there's still an aura of strippers and booze, but we've come a long way, baby! We've expanded our horizons, and today we are aware of options Hef never dreamed of (see *Smokin' Party Schemes* on page 128).

So, whether groom or best man, dream big. After all, this is not your grandfather's stag night, and, besides, why *should* the bride have all the fun?

— Christopher Measom

History of ...

The Stag Party

Stag: n [from Old English *stingan,* "to sting"] 1. an adult male red deer; *broadly*: the male of various deer 2. *chiefly Scot*: a young horse; *esp*: a young unbroken stallion 3. a male animal castrated after maturity 4. a young adult male domestic fowl 5. a social gathering of men only. **Stag**: adj (1843) 1. a: restricted to men (a ~ party) b: intended or suitable for a gathering of men only; *esp*: pornographic (~ movies)

Bachelor party, stag party, stag night, stag do, bulls' party, bucks' party, bucks' night—whatever you call it—this particular men-only celebration is thought to have its origins in ancient times. The story goes that the first stag shindig took place among Spartan soldiers who gathered one night to feast and drink a toast to a fellow warrior whose bachelor days were coming to an end. And by commemorating his impending marriage they marked his passage from childhood into adulthood.

It seems that not much has changed in the twenty-five hundred years that followed. Men assemble, drink and feast. Yes, somewhere between then and now paintball and strippers were added, but exactly when is not so clear. Some evidence exists that female "entertainment" has been around for at least the last hundred years. During the 19th century, bachelor farewells were mostly black-tie affairs—on the stodgy side—revolving around dinner, cigars and brandy. But there was one party that became so infamous—mostly due to the presence of a performer named "Little Egypt"—that it hounded the best man through the rest of his life, showing up in print whenever he did—including his obituary.

. . . Herbert Barnum Seeley came into prominence over six years ago through a dinner which he arranged for his brother, Clinton Barnum Seeley, who was married shortly afterward to Miss Florence Tuttle. The dinner took place at Sherry's on the night of Dec. 19, 1896, and when it was at its height was interrupted by the arrival of Police Captain Chapman, who arrested some of the diners and several women who were giving a vaudeville entertainment. . . .
—*The New York Times*, July 3, 1903

Herbert B. Seeley Dead.
Host of Famous "Seeley Dinner" and
Grandson of Late P. T. Barnum.
Herbert Barnum Seeley, a grandson of the late P. T. Barnum and the host of the "Seeley dinner" in 1896, died on Tuesday in Maine. . . . In December 1896, he gave a farewell bachelor dinner . . . Capt. Chapman . . . raided the dining room, giving as his excuse that he understood that indecent dances were to be given. . . .
—*The New York Times*, July 9, 1914

But the bachelor party as we tend to think of it today—wild drinking, stag films, wild women—seems to have appeared after World War II, or maybe not so much appeared as evolved from a uniquely upper-crust rite of passage to a mainstream one. Since the mid-20th century, the stag party has branched out even further (and perhaps grown up a bit too). Beyond the standard lap dances and all-night binges—not that there's anything wrong with that—many have chosen to do their male bonding in more creative or individual ways that take the groom's particular predilections into consideration (see page 128 for some ideas). And in most recent times, there came the bachelorette party. . . . But that is a stagette of a truly different color.

He left the party to have an orgy of his own.

The Sample

by Theo. Jordan

It was hotter than the hinges of hell in the room, but the shades were pulled all the way down, shutting out any trace of fresh air. Harry had pulled Joe away from one of the blinds, when he tried to open it a little. "You want the cops in here?" he had asked.

There were six of them altogether, in the one big room . . . the four guys and the two girls. All the guys except Joe were stripped down to their jockey shorts. Of the girls, plump, red-headed Rita, who was stretched out with Izzy on one of the coverless iron beds, was naked . . . she was very tight and giggling at something Izzy whispered in her ear, while he fondled the beanbag softness of her full breasts. Peggy, plati-num blonde and thinner, though still with plenty to show, was showing it as she bent over the alcohol-stained round table in room center, mixing herself a drink. All she had on were a pair of brief black lace panties.

"Hey, you creeps," she said, in her nasal, harsh voice, "we're out of ice again." She looked at her glass, half filled with vodka and flat ginger ale, in disgust, and pulled dripping fingers from the empty insulated bag.

"Jeest!" exclaimed Juan, who was sitting up on the other bed, scratching a sweating, hairy chest. "We gotta have ice. In this heat . . ."

Izzy said, "Aw, who gives a crap about ice?" He turned back to the nude, plump Rita and began kissing her damp neck. It seemed to Joe, sitting on the battered straight wooden chair by the bureau, that Rita and Izzy had been going at it all day, as they had all the night before.

Harry looked at Joe and said, "You wanna go out and get ice, Joey? You ain't doin' yourself or anybody else much good around here.

"Okay," said Joe. All of a sudden, he was glad to be get-ting out of there. When Harry and the guys were setting up the party, a couple of days before, he didn't see how he was going to be able to wait for it. These were real guys . . . Harry was married, though he wasn't living with his

wife, and Izzy and Juan had been around plenty . . . and this was going to be a real party. Not the nice-nelly dances he had known as a kid, not the fumbling sessions in the back of a car, or in some girl's living room . . . this was going to be a real bang-up, grown-up wingding.

The only trouble was, now that he was on it, he didn't fit. Last night, he had drunk too much, too fast, and passed out cold. Today, he felt too lousy even to take a cut with one of the girls. Besides, the idea of doing it in front of the rest of them froze him up tight, in spite of the heat.

Walking slowly down the street to the liquor store, he wondered what was wrong with him. He knew he wasn't queer . . . he had never had any trouble wanting girls before . . . but he knew he wasn't going to be able to make it, even when he got back to the

room. Not with those two girls . . . not with all the guys around. He thought about Alice, the tall, friendly girl he had left behind him when he came to Waterburg to take the assistant manager's job at the mill.

All at once, he had to call Alice, talk to her, hear the reassuring softness of her voice. He walked past the package store at the corner and entered the merciful air-conditioned coolness of a dimly lit saloon. Out of courtesy, not because he wanted it, he ordered a screwdriver, then went on back to the phone booth in the rear, pulling out silver from his pockets as he did so.

There was a girl phoning inside, and he waited for her to finish, leaning against the wall rack that held the telephone books. Thanks to the light in the booth, he could see that she was very pretty, her pert features soft-

ened by black curls that caught blue highlights from the booth light as she moved her head while talking. She was wearing a crisp white backless dress with red polka dots, and the smooth, golden-tan skin of her arms and back melted firmly into the fullness of her half-revealed breasts.

She opened the door and emerged, moving like a girl well aware that her body had a life of its own. She looked up at him through long, curling, black eyelashes and said, "I'm sorry . . . it's all yours now," and her voice was both firm and soft, like the rest of her. Joe was oddly pleased to discover that her dark curls came barely to his shoulder. He said, "It's okay . . . I didn't mind waiting," and entered the booth. The earphone was still warm from contact with her flesh.

Alice was out . . . not until he hung up and began plucking his returned quarters form the slot did Joe remember something in her last letter about going to the shore for a week. He opened the door and walked back toward the bar.

The girl was sitting on the next stool to the one in front of which his drink was set up. She was sipping a scotch mist. "Did you connect?" she asked casually.

He shook his head, took a sip of his screwdriver. "How about you?"

She shrugged, perilously in view of the strapless dress, but her full breasts supported the crisp fabric. "Sometimes," she said "you connect and wish you hadn't." She wrinkled her pert little nose charmingly and laughed silently, and he smelled the perfume she exuded like an invisible cloud of enchantment. "Now, I've got to have Sunday dinner with my aunt and she bores me silly," she said.

Her name was Monica, and she was even newer in town than Joe. She was still looking around for the right job. In the meantime, she was sharing an apartment on the edge of River Park, not far away, with another girl. "Ethel's away for the weekend," she said, "and I simply got lonely at the prospect of three whole days shut up there by myself. You probably think I'm terrible for coming into a place like this alone, but I had to be where there were people."

"On the contrary," Joe told her, "I think you're most attractive . . . the most attractive girl I've met since I got here."

She smiled her thanks, and they chatted, becoming increasingly at ease, while he bought her two more scotch mists, had another screwdriver himself. All at once, his hangover had faded, and he found himself enjoying life once more. He offered to

The Sample

buy her a third drink, but she refused.

"This is silly," she said. "Why waste money here at a bar, when we could buy a bottle and go to my place. It's not as cool as this, but at least there's a breeze from the river."

Monica's apartment was unexpectedly pleasant, even luxurious, in a new building with a sweeping picture-window view of the park and river, and the sunset over the low hills beyond. There was a breeze, but after the air-conditioned coolness of the bar, Joe found that his shirt was wringing wet. Monica, who had disappeared into one of the two bedrooms, emerged wearing brief white pique shorts and halter. She laid a palm on his back and it made a sopping sound that was almost a splash. "Poor dear!" she said, her dark,

luminous eyes looking softly down into his. "Why don't you take a shower while I mix us a drink, and let your things dry out in the bathroom? There's a terry-cloth robe hanging inside the door that's miles too big for me. You can wear that while they're drying. It's much too hot to worry about being conventional."

He stood under the cold water, letting it wash away the grime, visible and invisible, that the heat and dirt of the city, and the orgy he had taken leave of, had left in his pores and soul. He felt cleansed, inside and out, when he emerged. He decided not to towel off, lest the effort make him sweat again, to let the toweling robe do the chore instead. Climbing into it, he discovered that, while it might be miles too large for Monica, it was much too small for him. It bound his shoulders and he could barely wrap it across his lean belly and hips, while the bottom came barely below his knees.

When he emerged, Monica was curled enticingly in a corner of the sofa, looking out through the picture window, the drinks set out neatly on a coffee table in front of her. She gurgled with laughter when she saw him in the robe and said, "You look like something that's been pre-shrunk."

All at once, Joe felt embarrassment flood over him in a wave of heat. To cover his confusion, he reached for his drink, saw Monica extend an alluringly rounded brown arm for hers. "Cheers!" she said, and he had to look at her.

She was on her knees on the sofa, facing him and leaning toward him a little, so that he could not help but see almost the entirety of her bosom. The twin full firm globes seemed anxious to burst from the confinement of the skimpy white halter that barely contained them, and the valley between was deep and softly shadowed. In this position, her knees nudged his flank at the double-prow of thighs whose satin firmness bespoke her triumphant youth and health. Her shorts were almost invisible, trapped in the crease of her body, and he could see the top of her navel peeping out at him above their waistband.

He drank deeply, without being able to take his eyes from her, then said as he put down his glass, "Careful, Monica . . . I'm a man, and I'm all too human."

"Are you?" she said softly, insinuatingly, her eyes holding his like twin radar beams locked on a target. "Are you, Joe? I was beginning to wonder."

He twisted his torso toward hers, and she moved a little further forward. Their lips met and seemed to flow together, and once again he was aware of the sweet allure of her perfume. Not until they pulled apart, so that she could assume a more comfortable position, did Joe become aware that the ridiculous robe had been so pulled awry that it left him, for all practical purposes, fully exposed.

Instinctively, he made a quick move to pull it back together, but her hands gripped his wrists, and she said, "I'm not worried about you now, dear. Don't forget, I'm a woman . . . and human, too." Then gripping him tightly, she pulled him to his feet and led him toward one of the two bedrooms beyond. "It will be better in here," she whispered hoarsely, her voice vibrant with desire . . .

When the madness at last left him limp and exhausted, Monica was still nuzzling him, and the

The Sample

striped sky visible through the Venetian blinds was already dark. All he could murmur was, "Golly, Darling!" He sat up and ran a hand through his damp hair, shook himself like a dog emerging from the sea.

She sat up beside him, ran smooth fingers through her dark crop of curls and smiled at him affectionately. "I hope you won't think too badly of me, Joe," she said, growing suddenly serious, even a little sad of face. "I know how it is with a man . . . once you've had one of us, you lose interest."

"Not me," said Joe fervently. "When can I see you again?"

"Whenever you want to," she said simply. "You're very sweet."

"Not as sweet as you," he replied.

"Oh come!" she said, laughing softly. "Let's not be sickening about this."

When he got back to the party, the fetid heat struck him like a blow on the face as he pushed through the door that Harry, still stripped to his shorts, unlocked for him after hearing his voice. Harry had an unlit cigarette drooping from his lower lip, and he squinted at Joe a bit blearily, then stepped aside to let him pass, saying, "For Chrissakes, where you been, kid?"

Joe said, "Oh, I went for a walk," as casually as he could.

Harry rubbed both hands diagonally across his dripping flanks. "Some walk!" he said. "You musta done twenty miles. You been gone over four hours!"

Behind him, Izzy and Rita, stark naked, lay asleep on the farther bed. Juan sat on the other, his back against the wall, snoring with an empty glass in one hand. Peg, still wearing the black panties, was leaning with

her back to the table, juggling a drink, looking neither the better nor worse for wear since Joe's departure earlier.

She said, "Joe don't like us. I bet he found a broad of his own somewhere."

Once again, Joe felt embarrassment sweep over him in a wave of heat. He saw Harry's bloodshot eyes narrow as he regarded him, heard Peg say, "Looka him blush! I musta scored a bulls-eye. Where'd you find her, Joey-boy? Come on . . . tell us."

"Yeah, kid . . . what gives?" asked Harry aggressively. "I thought we were supposed to be on this weekend together. Don't be so selfish."

"I'm not being selfish," Joe protested. "Nothing happened." He pushed past them to the table, poured himself a drink and got it down.

"I know one way to find out if he's been with a broad," said Peg, her dull blue eyes lighting up at the prospect. "And I'm the little girl who's gonna find out. Besides, Joey's fair game. He's been avoidin' us all weekend like we was poison or somethin'. Come on, sweetie-pie . . . let's see if there's any life left in you."

"Okay," said Joe realizing he was licked and hating himself for it. "I did meet a girl."

"Whadja do with her, Joey . . . give her a great big gooey kiss?" Peg asked derisively. "maybe you're all wore out from holdin' hands."

Joe took another drink and discovered that his hands were trembling. He said, "We went to bed together," then added quickly, "but it wasn't what you think."

"So now it takes thought." Peg moved up beside him at the table and poured herself another. "You pick up some floozie and go to bed with her, when you won't even give a tumble to Rita or me that you've been properly introduced to. Jeest! It's time you got a lesson in manners."

Before he could move, Peg was on him, pulling his clothing from him, snarling like an animal. The last thing he was aware of before she pushed him onto the bed was a button popping loose from his soaking wet shirt and Harry laughing like a devil in the background. Then he heard Peg, savagely upon him, cry triumphantly, "See? She didn't use him all up . . ."

Monica was cooking eggs and bacon in the kitchenette when her roommate Ethel walked in. Ethel, a taller girl with long ash-blonde hair, a strong, handsome face and a strong, handsome figure, looked the apartment over before joining Monica in the kitchenette. "So you had a man up here," she said. "Did he pay off?"

Monica shook her dark curls and Ethel said, "How the hell we gonna pay the rent here if we don't get some business soon. We musta been crazy to leave Chicago."

"Don't worry," said Monica. "This will pay off. This is a kid with a lot of friends . . . got a real good job at the mill. By the time he gets through telling them about me, we'll be in business . . . plenty."

"Okay, if it works out," said Ethel, pouring herself a drink. "But no more free samples, hear? We aren't in business for our health. No more samples."

"Okay," said Monica, picking up the spatula to lift the eggs from the pan. 🐌

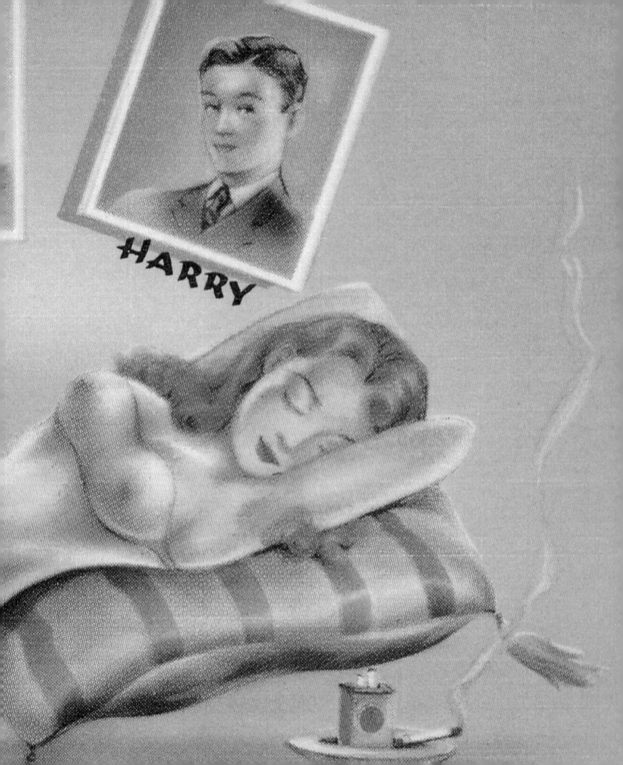

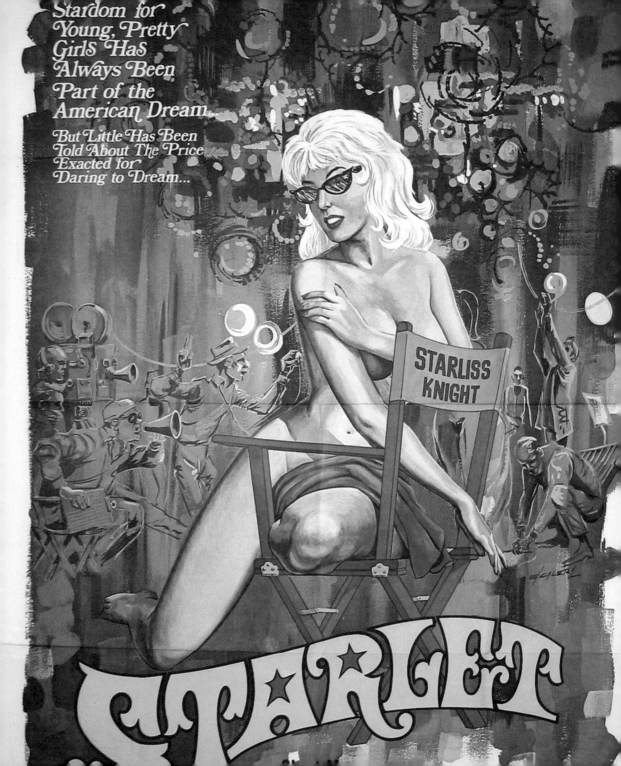

History of . . .
The Stag Film

During wartime, a valiant musketeer

presents himself, famished, at the door

of an inn. "Nothing left to eat," answers

the innkeeper. Happily, thanks to an

accommodating servant girl, an amorous

meal is offered him. He enjoys it so much

that, on the appearance of another girl,

he demands a second helping.

—Ado Kyrou's description of the 1908 film *A l'Ecu d'Or ou*

la Bonne Auberge (At the Golden Shield or the Good Inn)

Although the evidence is sparse, it seems that the pioneer stag filmmakers working during the first decade of the twentieth century were French. And according to a series of articles titled "The History of Sex in Cinema," which ran in *Playboy* magazine in the 1960s, "By the end of *la belle époque* no self-respecting brothel in any of the large cities on the Continent considered its facilities complete without a stock of these films." Buenos Aires, it seems, was also a great producer and shower of stag films. In Eugene O'Neill's *Bound East for Cardiff* (1916), the character Yank says to his pal Driscoll, "D'yuh remember the times we had in Buenos Aires? The movin' pictures in Barracas? Some class to them, d'yuh remember?"

O'Neill later said, "Those pictures were mighty

rough stuff. Nothing was left to the imagination. Every form of perversity was enacted and, of course, the sailors flocked to them."

Thus the erotic spectacles formerly enacted in brothels during the eighteenth and nineteenth centuries to "stimulate" the clientele were replaced by modern media—the moving picture—and America would not be left behind.

A Free Ride—a 1915 film about a man who picks up two girls and takes them for a "drive" in the country—is the earliest extant American stag film. In America, however, because brothels were not as common or as regulated as in Europe, the stag found other outlets.

From the twenties into the fifties, the largest market for stag films in America remained men-only "smokers" or "stag parties," and the audience most commonly belonged to two kinds of male groups: voluntary social organizations (Legionnaires, Shriners, Elks), and college students, usually those in fraternities. Although officially illegal, these showings were invariably tolerated as a necessary ritual of masculine emergence. (In Bloomington, Indiana, the local Legion even announced their next stag screening in the hometown newspaper.) The law not only turned a blind eye to these occasions, but even participated. Policemen, in particular, often having access to confiscated prints, shared in the stag rituals.

After World War II, the French stag again came to the forefront and was admired as *la pièce de résistance* of the genre. Two outstanding examples are *Petit Conte de Noël* (1950) and *La Femme au Portrait* (1952).

British films of the 1960s piqued stag interest on several levels: they often involved settings

MOVIE VIEWER SPECIAL
FOR TITAN CUSTOMERS
ONLY $4.95

DON'T MISS a thrill, a breath-taking, tantalizing action in Titan Stag Films. New Optic Movie Viewer for 8mm - 50′ films gives big, bright, life-like motion pictures for intimate shows; even slow or stop motion.

MEN...YOU GET ALL TEN OF THESE TERRIFIC STAG MOVIE SUBJECTS FOR LESS THAN THE PRICE OF ONE!

Moment of Bliss

2. Savage Delights

Fanny Makes Good

4. Beautiful Animal

Secret Passions

6. Made In France

Lost Inhibitions

8. Boudoir Frantics

Forbidden Fruit

10. Coming Out Party

You must be delighted...you must be thrilled...you must agree that these are the most terrific girls you've ever seen in action or your money back!

TEN STAG MOVIE SUBJECTS

all ten only **$2.00**

8mm

GREATEST ADULT MOVIE BARGAIN EVER!

A once-in-a-lifetime opportunity for you to get ten delightfully different, sensationally thrilling stag shows on film FOR LESS THAN THE PRICE OF ONE! Lovely, luscious young beauties go all out to please...ten girls, ten action plots, ten exclusive stag subjects, the kind you've always wanted, the kind only Titan Stag Films gives you!

NOW! DON'T DELAY! SPECIAL LIMITED INTRO-DUCTORY OFFER FOR NEW CUSTOMERS ONLY!

RUSH $2 CASH, CHECK OR MONEY ORDER (FOR 16mm SEND $4.50)

DEPT. D-11

TITAN STAG FILMS

STRAIGHT FROM THE
ORIGINALS
THOSE SHOCKING
THOSE INTIMATE

STAG STORIES

A fantastic opportunity to obtain a daring, privitely printed edition featuring those rare stag story favorites you used to pass along on typewritten pages. Some you'll remember, many you've never seen, all in their original form. Every detail intact, every description vivid. They'll leave you breathless!

MANY WITH ARTIST ILLUSTRATIONS

FABULOUS PHOTOS YOU'LL NEVER FORGET!

THE MIDGET AND THE DUCHESS • THE YOUNG LADY AND HER DOG • I WAS CAPTIVE TO SIX WOMEN • DAY IN LIFE OF A TRAVELING SALESMAN • SHE STOOPS TO CONQUER, and many others, each more sensational than the next. Guaranteed!

ADULTS ONLY

Sent in Plain Wrapper. Rush cash, check or money order; no COD's!

SENSATIONAL PRICE LIMITED EDITION

1.98 ppd.

PRIVATE EDITIONS
Mailing Address
BOX 46856, DEPT K-11
LOS ANGELES 46, CALIFORNIA

more elaborate than the traditional stag, and they began to stress "kinky" sexual behavior, like sado-masochism and "buggery." And when pornography was legalized in Denmark in 1968, the result was a spate of films of a higher technical quality than any that had preceded it.

America, perhaps due to the availability of amateur filmmaking equipment and its puritanical roots, retained its entirely less polished, more amateurish esthetic.

The stag era—if not the stag film itself—ended with the emergence of the publicly screened hardcore film around 1970. Despite some weakening of the genre through its more open and available screening, the stag film and its variants, it seems, are not about to disappear. Its freeing affirmation of the pleasures of the body combined with a lack of social consequences, its open acceptance of our common human needs, let us forget for a while that man does not live by head alone.

—Excerpted from *Dirty Movies*
by Al Di Lauro and Gerald Rabkin

Although the majority of stag films after World War II abandoned any pretense of story line in favor of simple striptease (and/or dancing whores in general), earlier films revolved around these five common plots described by William Rotsler in his 1974 book *Contemporary Erotic Cinema*:

Plot 1.   Handling some phallic-shaped object arouses a woman alone at home, masturbation follows. A man arrives, is invited inside, sexual play begins.

Plot 2.   A farm girl gets excited watching animals copulate. She runs into a farmhand, or a traveling salesman, and sexual play begins.

Plot 3.   A doctor begins examining a woman and sexual play begins.

Plot 4.   A burglar finds a girl in bed and has his way with her or vice versa.

Plot 5.   A sunbather or skinny-dipper gets caught and seduced.

STAG PARTY CLASSICS

42 SETS OF 12 PHOTOS
BIG 504 TOTAL ALL FOR ONLY $1.00

Spicy photos for adults... the kind that'll make an artist blush. Full-blown beauties. Front, back, top, bottom... every position revealed in breathtaking detail. Why pay 500x more? Satisfaction guaranteed or money back. Rush $1 to: **Sensational Photo Offer** Box 46744, Hollywood 46, Calif., Dept. AA-11

FIGURE MODEL PHOTOS

STAG PARTY ORIGINALS

Authentic, unretouched stags of well known gals before they reached the top. Rare thrillers all.

MOVIES, 8mm—50'.... $3
MOVIES, 16mm—100'.. $6
SLIDES, 5—2 x 2's.... $2
PHOTOS, 8—4 x 5's.. $2

BERNARD OF HOLLYWOOD
Box 46977, Dept. 1411, Los Angeles 46, Cal.

STAG FILM FAVORITES

AFRICAN INTRUDER (1960–65), AMOROUS LESBIANS (1966), SUPER SALESMAN, THE ARABIAN, THE ART OF LOVE (1930s), ATOMIC JAZZER (1946–51), AUTOMATIC BUTT (aka Three Pals), AVEC SES PIEDS (With His Feet, France, 1946), BACHELOR AND THE MAID (1950–56), BANANA SPLIT (aka Jane's Masseur), BASHFUL BOY, BASHFUL FISHERMAN, BAT MAN (1964–66), BEACH BUGGERY (1967–69), BEARDED VIBRATOR (1966), BEATNICK BEDLAM (1966), THE BELLBOY, (1930–35), BIG AND LONG (1960–63), BIG AND WHITE (1960–63), BIG BAD BILL (aka Rod Rammer), BIG BOY (aka Mexican Big Dick), BIG DADDY, BIG SISTER, BIG SURPRISE (1970), BISEXUAL BUGGERY (1968–70), BLACK HOSE (aka Take My Daughter!), BLONDIE MAKES GOOD (aka Motel Moderne), BREAKING IN BLONDIE (1947–48), BRING YOUR TOOL (aka The Handyman), BROTHER JOHN, BURGLAR BOY (1948–52), BUSY LESBIAN CLUB (1930s), CASTING COUCH (1924), WHO IS MARY POPPIN'?, CHASTITY BELT (aka The Locksmith), CHINA DOLL (1959–62), CHINA GIRL (1960–65), CHINESE DELIVERY BOY (aka Black Market), CIRCUS (aka Burlesque Queen), CLAM BAKE, CLEAN-CUT TRUCK DRIVER (1964–66), CLOSELY RELATED (1965–66), CLOSET (aka While the Cat's Away),

COCKEYED PORTER (1947–48), **COEDS IN SCHOOL**, **COLLEGE COED** (aka The Nun's Story), **COLLEGE TUITION A GO-GO** (1964–66), **CONFIDENTIAL CIRCUS** (1930–35), **COUNTRY COUSIN** (1962–64), **DARKIE RHYTHM** (1932–35), **DETECTIVE ONE HUNG LOW**, (1948–52), **DILDO DELIGHT** (1968–70), **DR. FIX 'EM** (1958–62), **DR. HARDON'S INJECTIONS** (1931–36), **DR. LONGPETER** (1948–55), **DO UNTO OTHERS** (aka Rape in Reverse), **EAGER BEAVER** (1958–64), **THE EXCLUSIVE SAILOR** (1920s), **FANNY FROM FRISCO** (1958–61), **FARMER'S DAUGHTER** (1930s), **FLAT TIRE** (1940s), **FORCED ENTRY** (1970), **FORREST FRIENDS** (1968–70), **FOREVER LIMBER** (1935–39), **FOUR ON A PONY** (1967), **FOUR ON THE FLOOR** (aka Four Way Swap, 1966–67), **FOXY FIREMAN** (1956–60), **FRENCH MAID** (1968), **FUCK ME FUCK MY FRIENDS** (1968), **FUZZY WAZZY THE REPAIRMAN** (1968), **G.I. JOE RETURNS HOME** (1951–54), **GIRL FARM** (1968–70), **GIRLS WILL BE BOYS**, **GOING DOWN** (1930s), **HARLEM HONEY**, **HARRY LAYS TWO** (1968–70), **THE HAT CHECK GIRL** (1965–66), **HAVE CRACK WILL SHACK** (1964–66), **HILLBILLIES' FROLICS** (1930s), **HIPPIES FLOWER PARTY** (1967–68), **HOT CHICKS** (1947–48), **HOT PANTIES** (1966–67), **HOT PARTY** (1928–33), **HOT PUSSY** (1930s), **HOUSE CALL** (aka The Nympho), **HOW DEEP IS MY VALLEY** (1965), **THE HYPNOTIST** (1932), **THE ICEMAN** (1920s), **THE INSURANCE SALESMAN** (1967), **IRENE GETS AN IDEA** (1967), **JACK THE SNIFFER** (1964–66). . .

.Love is the answer, but

while you're waiting for the

answer, sex raises some

pretty good questions

—Woody Allen

^{MORE!} STAG FILM FAVORITES

. . . **JAPANESE MAGICIAN** (aka An Oriental's Dream), **JOHNNY TWATSUCKER** (c. 1965), **KEEP IT KINKY** (1968), **KKK NIGHTRIDERS** (1939), **KRAZY KAT HOUSE, LADY BARBER** (c. 1964), **LADY BURGLAR** (1966), **LADY DOCTOR** (c. 1952), **LATEX SALESMAN** (1958), **THE LECHEROUS TAILOR** (1970), **LESBIAN CANDLE** (1968), **LITTLE EVA** (1920s), **LONG AND WHITE** (c. 1961), **LONG JOHN AND TIGHT MARY** (c. 1947), **LOVE GAME, LOVE HUNGRY** (1950s), **LOVE SLAVE** (1966), **LUCKY BOYS** (1968), **LUCKY PILOT** (aka The Aviator), **LUCKY PROWLER** (c. 1968), **THE MASKED MUFF DIVERS** (aka Rin-Tin-Tin Mexicano, 1930s), **MEXICAN MIX UP** (1945), **MR. FIXIT** (aka The Electrician), **MODERN GIGOLO** (1928), **MODERN PIRATES** (1930s), **MORTIMER THE SALESMAN** (c.1940), **NIGHT IN A TURKISH HAREM** (1920s), **OF COURSE SPUNKY** (aka Dancing Teacher), **OH DOCTOR!** (1930s), **DR. PENIS** (c. 1950), **O' MY PUSSY** (1970), **0069 THE MAN FROM UNCLE** (c. 1965), **OPHELIA'S WAY** (aka Pricking Cherries) (c. 1964), **ORGY AND BESS,** (c. 1964) **OVER HERE, ROVER** (c. 1964), **PECKER HEAD FROLICS** (1930s), **PEG'S PARTY** (c. 1960), **THE PERVERTED DENTIST** (1970), **PETER THE MEATER EATER** (aka Peter the Meter Reader), **THE PLUMBER** (1930s), **THE PLUMBER'S HELPER** (c. 1962), **THE PLUMBER'S SON** (1950s), **PRICK TEASER PARTS I AND II** (c. 1965), **THE PSYCHIATRIST** (c. 1965), **PSYCHO**

SEX (c. 1969), **PUNISHMENT FOR NAUGHTY GIRLS** (1968), **PUSSY CLUB** (c. 1966), **RADIO REPAIRMAN** (c. 1948), **RANDY INTRUDER** (c. 1968), **RASCAL REX** (1930s), **REAR ADMIRAL** (1960s), **REAR VIEW** (1960s), **ROOM SERVICE** (c. 1960), **RUB DOWN** (c. 1959), **SALES LADY** (1953), **THE SALESMAN AND THE VIRGIN** (c. 1965), **THE SANDWICH** (c. 1969), **SANTA'S DREAM** (aka Santa's Ramrod, c. 1964), **SATAN'S CHILDREN** (1968), **SCHOOLGIRL INITIATION** (1968), **SCHOOL GIRL LUST** (1966), **SCHOOL OF HARD COCKS** (1967–69), **SECRETARY GETS A RAISE** (aka Tillie the Toiler, 1940s), **SHOE COBBLER** (1930s), **SNOW WHITE AND THE CUTIE** (animated cartoon, 1950s), **SPUNK ORGY** (1968), **STAG SHOW** (1958), **STRIP POKER** (1956), **SUBURBAN WIFE** (1966), **SUCK-A-GO-GO** (1968), **SUSIE SWINGS IT** (1966), **SWAP** (1968), **SWEDISH MASSAGE, SWINGING DEBS** (1965), **TARZAN AND BOY** (1950s), **THIS GUN FOR HIRE** (1949–52), **THREE IS A CROWD** (1968), **THREE IS NOT A CROWD** (aka Twat Time, 1965), **THREE OF A KIND** (aka Fruit Salad), **TORTILLA GIRLS** (1948), **TORTURE OF THE TICKLING TONGUES** (1930s), **TWO BACHELORS AND THE MAID, TWO BUGS AND TWO BUNNIES, TWO COLORED LONG JOHNS AND WHITE BEAUTY** (aka Two Nights and a Day, 1950–55), **TWO INTO ONE** (1968), **THE UNDERTAKER'S DREAM** (1968), **UP AND DOWN** (aka Sex Plantation), **WHAT THE BUTLER SAW AND DID** (1965), **YOU ASKED FOR IT** (1956–62), **YOU'RE NOT GOING TO STICK THAT IN ME** (aka The Honeymoon), **YUM YUM GIRL** (1963–65)!

BEING THE BEST BEST MAN
Advice for

The whole idea behind stag night (or day or long weekend) is to go beyond simple fun to arrive at a higher plain—the plain of male bonding. It's about friendship and camaraderie with, perhaps, a little rivalry (or team building) mixed in, and can be achieved through the use of jokes, gags and game playing, or even working as a group to, let's say, install a new kitchen in the groom's (and bride's) home.

No matter what form your stag celebration takes, the first and foremost priority of the best man (as organizer) is to take the bachelor into account and make sure it's a memorable party for him—in a good way. The second priority is to make sure everything goes well. As the man in charge—the leader of the evening—you are the one who will get things started and keep them going. You are the go-to man who will know who's coming, what happens next and how to pay. You will also, if necessary, nip any brewing brawls in the bud, make sure your guys aren't overly aggressive to the entertainment (be nice to the stripper/dwarf/sex clown) and last, make sure everyone gets around safely.

"The bridegroom's been trying to get you on the 'phone all morning—something to do with bail."

CHECKLIST

BEFORE (Organize)

❏ Talk to the groom and decide who's coming—and who isn't—choose a mix of players who get along.

❏ Find out what kind of send-off he wants (where, what kinds of activities).

❏ Secretly add a surprise element (a dwarf boxing match, his high-school gym teacher who is now a stripper . . . use your imagination).

❏ Decide on the budget (What can your invitees afford?).

❏ With the budget in mind, decide on what the evening (or day or weekend) will be and when: an at-home party, bar-hopping, day of golf, zorbing getaway, road trip to Mexico (keep in mind that the night before the wedding is never a good idea; try to shoot for at least two weeks before).

❏ Collect funds needed for the evening in advance (i.e. the entertainment, an open bar, the dinner, the venue rental, the paintball game).

❏ Once guest list, budget and dates are settled, sort out and arrange the details—from food to entertainment to herding a gaggle of guys around.

DURING (Preserve and Protect)

❏ Make sure the groom survives—and is in good shape for the wedding. No dyeing of body parts that will show in the wedding photos, no shaving of body parts that will show in the wedding photos, no bruises or stitches that will show in the wedding photos . . . most of all, do not lose track of the groom.

AFTER (Obfuscate)

❏ Being mysterious about all that went on during the stag celebration is a good idea—those who did not attend need to know nothing. (See "Obfuscation" tips on page 174.)

DOWN AND DIRTY RULES

1. The groom spends no money.

2. The groom gets very little information beforehand (where and when to show up is usually enough).

3. No photos (following the traditional code of silence—or at least a decent attempt at muddying the waters—can never go wrong).

4. Make sure there is safe transportation for everyone.

5. Make it memorable, make it fun.

"I thought this was to be a party for Men Only!"

39

EROTIC DANCERS 101

Because this is not exactly the most up-and-up business and you can't ask for recommendations from your accountant (although it's worth a try), the rule is "buyer beware."

You will find an abundance of strippers online with one quick Google search, many of whom are individual strippers working from home. There are also many agencies that will act as a go-between and can provide more stability and credibility than individual "artists." Either way, like any business transaction, be clear about what you want and what is offered. Most of all—be creative. Work with the agency or dancer to throw around ideas to come up with a more tailored entertainment experience. *Have fun.*

HIRE

- Know what you want (mild or spicy).

- Ask for references.

- Negotiate ahead of time. The first price you get may not be the best.

- Find out what the stripper(s) look like beforehand and make sure that's what you want. Many sites display amazing model-ready images that don't, unfortunately, represent anyone who works there.

- Choose the dancer you want and one or two alternates. Sometimes the stripper you want won't be available on the night of the party.

- Get everything in writing.

RULES

- Treat them with respect
- No pinching, biting, slapping, licking, or verbal abuse
- No touching without explicit permission from the dancer

PRICING GUIDELINES

- Figure around $200 for the first hour—but this can be just the cost of getting the stripper to the party. If you want her to strip, then often it's all about the tips, so make sure you ask exactly what is included in the price and what is expected as far as tips.

TIPPING TIPS

- All strippers work for tips. No tips = no fun.
- $40–$50 per person tip is standard (be sure to have small bills on hand).

SUCCESS TIPS

- Play nice
- Give generously
- No photos

FIRST-TIME BEST MAN EXOTIC DANCER CHECKLIST

❏ **CHECK IN WITH THE STAG** Do some research and give the guy some options. Find out what he wants and make sure that's what he gets.

❏ **CHECK THE CHECK** Find out how much this is going to cost and how many guys are chipping in. Then adjust your budget from there. Recontact the bachelor to readjust his expectations if necessary.

❏ **SEEK A STRIPPER** Allow a minimum of two weeks to find the right stripper/bachelor/budget fit. The more time you allow, the more choices you will have in the end.

❏ **SET UP** Make sure there's a place for the stripper to get ready (a bathroom will usually do), and ask in advance what kinds of props she'll need (a chair, a rope, a paddle).

❏ **PASS THE PLATE** Collect the stripper's fee beforehand and arrange to pay the stripper half when she arrives, the rest when the show is over (to insure she fulfills her contract). Be sure to tell the guys that tipping is the best way to get a great show (one dollar bills are fine, fives even better, tens and twenties should get you quite a show).

❏ **OUR POLE IS YOUR POLE** Make the girl feel at home and relaxed. Being excessively aggressive is a sure way to end the show early. If there's food and drink around, be neighborly and offer some to the dancer and her bodyguard/driver/helper/staff.

❏ **GOOD STRIPPERS GONE BAD** If things aren't turning out as you agreed—she's late, she's not what you arranged—feel free to turn her away or renegotiate. But be fair; it's not about saving money at the last minute, it's about everyone fulfilling their obligations.

❏ **CUSTOMIZE** When the stripper arrives, give her guidance on what you'd like her to do with the bachelor—special clothes to dress him in, key phrases to use, specific names she should mention.

43

SIGNET 35¢ BOOKS

the Bachelor Party

BY

Paddy Chayefsky

A NEW MOTION PICTURE
BY THE AUTHOR OF THE
BROADWAY HIT
MIDDLE OF THE NIGHT

The Bachelor Party

A Screenplay by Paddy Chayefsky

INTERIOR. THE OFFICE

We look down on the bookkeeping department. All the desks are occupied but two. There are six women and our three men. The office is silent with industry, everybody's head bent over his desk. There is the occasional punctuation of an adding machine or a typewriter or a phone ringing.

Our three men are bent over their tally sheets, worksheets, and ledgers, occasionally reaching up to quickly tabulate something on the adding machine. After a moment, Walter says;

WALTER: (*without looking up from his work*) You fellows going to Arnold's party tonight?

KENNETH: (*without looking up*) No, I'm not going, are you?

WALTER: No. Eddie already hooked me for four bucks for Arnonld's present. This dinner is going to cost another couple of good dollars.

CHARLIE: It looks like nobody's going to Arnold's bachelor party.

WALTER: You ain't going?

CHARLIE: No, I'm not going.

WALTER: Eddie's going to be mad.

CHARLIE: I told Eddie last week I couldn't make it. I've got school. Eddie's a bachelor. It's all right for him to go rooting around town, picking up girls.

WALTER: Yeah, you get married you give that kind of thing up.

KENNETH: Yeah, Charlie says Eddie has a whole bunch of chorus girls lined up for us tonight.

Walter's head comes up for the first time.

WALTER: No kidding.

CHARLIE: I didn't say that. I just said that if I knew Eddie, we'd probably wind up with some of his crazy girl friends.

Walter looks back down to his work again.

KENNETH: I don't know were he gets all these girls. He's a screwy looking jerk.

WALTER: Did you see that blonde who was up here looking for him last week?

KENNETH: Yeah. He told me she was a television actress. I think I saw her once on

The Bachelor Party

"Studio One." She was in a coal mine with some stir-crazy coalminer who was trying to strangle her with a necktie.

WALTER: I'd like to strangle her with a necktie.

KENNETH: Now, Walter, an old married man like you, with asthma and everything.

Walter looks up suddenly from his work, a strange sting of pain crossing his face.

WALTER: I get real jealous of Eddie sometimes. He's as free as a bird. Did you see that convertible he's got?

KENNETH: Yeah, he really banged it up I hear.

WALTER: You ought to see the old heap I've got. He walks out of here on payday, he can spend the whole works on having himself a good time. I walk out of here, and I got three kids and a wife, all of them with their palms out. I lost two bucks playing poker at my house last week. It was an economic catastrophe. My wife didn't sleep all night.

CHARLIE: He's late again.

WALTER: He'll be twenty minutes late again. If Flaherty walked in now, he'd fire him. If that ever happened to me, I think I'd kill myself. What does Eddie care? So he scrambles around for another job. Falherty told me last week I had too many days off. I told him I was sick in bed. What do you want me to do?

He turns back again to his work, his face

creased with anxiety. The three men work silently for a moment. Then the office door opens, and a man of about thirty-five, a little stout, but rather casual in his dress, wearing steel-rimmed glasses, enters. This is Eddie Watkins, the office bachelor. He seems to have had very little sleep the night before. His eyes, behind the wire-rimmed glasses, are heavy-lidded. A cigarette dangles listlessly from his mouth. There is something of the bacchanalian libertine about Eddie. There is a perfunctory exchange of hellos and good mornings, establishing that this is Eddie. He shuffles with ineffable weariness to his desk.*

WALTER: Hi, Eddie, you're early today, only twenty minutes late, what happened?

EDDIE: (*muttering through reluctant lips*) Flaherty come in yet?

KENNETH: No.

Eddie sits down at his desk, puffs his cigarette automatically for a moment. Then he reaches over to a pile of telephone directories on the floor beside his desk, pulls up the Manhattan one, flips through the pages, finding the number he wants. He picks up the phone.

EDDIE: Mary, give me an outside line. . . . (*he pauses, checks the number in the phone book again, dials, waits*) Hello, is this Leathercraft on Madison Avenue? . . . This is Mr. Watkins. I was in about a week ago. I ordered a military set and a wallet. They were supposed to be ready yesterday. . . . Yes, please, would you? . . . (*he is searching his pockets while he waits, finds a piece of paper, pulls it out*) Yeah, a military set and a wallet. . . .

WALTER: Is that what we bought poor Arnold?

EDDIE: (*on phone*) That's right. The following inscriptions should be on them: (*reads from the paper*) On the military set: "To Arnold: Best wishes on your marriage from Alice, Charlie, Eddie, Evelyn, Jeanette with two t's, Kenneth, Lucy, Mary, Olga, Walter, and Flaherty." Now on the wallet . . . Yeah, what? . . . Yeah, that's right—Flaherty. Now, on the wallet, the following inscription: "To my Best Friend Arnold from his Best Man Eddie." . . . No, to *my* best friend Arnold. . . . That's right. "From *his* best *man* Eddie" . . . Now, can I come in at lunch and pick them up? . . .

A young woman comes into the office, goes to Walter's desk and drops some papers before him.

WALTER: What's this, Jeanette?

GIRL: It's from finance, don't ask me.

This is the girl in the office who goes to the water cooler three times a morning and all the men covertly watch her. She is cute, but attractive more by comparison to the other women in the office. Nevertheless, all the

men, *including Eddie and Charlie, let their eyes cautiously watch her as she leaves, her sheath dress tight on her hips.*

Eddie, who has hung up, now rubs his eyes with two fingers to clear his head and picks up the phone again.

EDDIE: (*on phone*) Mary, give me the Hotel Westmore. Circle 7-0598.

CHARLIE: (*hands Kennie paper*) This isn't for me—it's for you.

EDDIE: (*to the others*) Now who owes me on the presents? Charlie, you owe me?

CHARLIE: I gave you four bucks yesterday. . . .

KENNETH: I owe you, Eddie. I'll pay you tomorrow, payday.

EDDIE: (on phone) Miss Frances Kelley, please. I think it's room 417. . . .

The three heads around him look slowly up from their respective work, naked interest manifest on their faces.

EDDIE: (*calling to one of the women in the office*) Hey, Evelyn, you owe me four bucks.

EVELYN: (*calling back*) All right. I know.

EDDIE: (on phone) Hello, Frances, this is Eddie. . . . All right, wait a minute. Give me a chance to explain. . . . I know I woke you up. . . . All right, let me tell you. You know I'm supposed to be the best man at this fellow

The Bachelor Party

Arnold's wedding. So I called him up last night because I didn't know whether I was supposed to wear tuxedo or tails. Well, he didn't know either, so he said: "Come on over to my girl's house with me tonight. They're making all the arrangements for the wedding now." So I called you and left a message at the desk saying I couldn't get over till about ten o'clock. . . . All right! That's what I'm going to explain! . . . Thank you. (*holds receiver against his chest and looks at his colleagues with air of a man being tried just a little too much. Returns receiver to his ear, listens for a moment*) All right, so I had to go over to Arnold's girl's house with Arnold last night. Well, there was about thirty people there, and, man, you never saw such a crazy mess. There was this little bald-headed guy there. He's the bride's uncle. He's come all the way down from Boston with his whole family to go to the wedding. The only trouble was, he wasn't invited. Well, this crazy uncle, he grabs ahold of me, he starts shaking me by the lapels. So I said: "What do you want from me? I ain't the groom! I'm just trying to find out whether I'm supposed to wear tuxedo or tails." (*apparently this got a laugh. Eddie breaks into a smile*) Funny, huh? . . . Look, Frances. I have to go to work now. I'm calling you from the office. How about letting me make this up to you?

I'll take you out to dinner Saturday night. . . . I can't make it tonight. The bachelor party's tonight. . . . All right, Saturday night. . . . It's a date. . . . S'help me. . . . I swear, right on time. Eight-thirty, okay? . . . Okay, we'll have a ball. Good-bye, go back to sleep.

He hangs up. The three married men look down again, to their ledgers and tap away again on their adding machines. Eddie sits slumped in his seat for a moment.

EDDIE: What did I just tell that girl, Saturday night?

KENNETH: Yeah.

EDDIE: (*picks up phone*) Mary, give me Columbus 5-1098. . . . What do you mean personal calls! These are business calls! Well, stop listening to other people's conversations. . . . What have you got, stock in the company? Columbus 5-1098. (*waits*)

KENNETH: Listen, Eddie, I don't think I can go tonight. My father-in-law's in from Akron, Ohio, and——

EDDIE: (*all sweetness*) Hello, who is this, Mrs. Stebbins? . . . This is Eddie, Mrs. Stebbins. I wonder if I can talk to Muriel. . . . Could I speak to her? . . . Thank you. . . .

The three married men each look up slowly again, naked envy on each face.

EDDIE: (*on phone*) Muriel, baby, listen, sweetie, I can't make it Saturday night. . . . I'm all loused up with this wedding I'm supposed to be the best man at. . . . We have to rehearse the ceremony. You'd think they were getting married on television. . . . Yes, sweetie, why don't I call you Monday. Maybe, we'll work out something before you go back to California. . . . All right, sweetie, good-bye.

He hangs up, sits a moment, then finally removes the cigarette from his mouth, crushes it in his ash tray, and turns to the others.

EDDIE: Well, what do you say? I'm going to call Louie and make a reservation for a table for tonight. Who's coming and who isn't? Walter, you're coming, right? It won't cost you more than three-fifty for the whole meal. What do you say, Walter? You only live once.

WALTER: (*strangely sad*) That's right. You only live once.

EDDIE: Well, yes or no?

WALTER: All right, I'll come.

EDDIE: Kennie?

KENNETH: Yeah, I'll get out of the house for a change.

EDDIE: How about you, Charlie?

Charlie is frowning down at a sheaf of adding machine totals in front of him.

CHARLIE: I don't think so, Eddie.

KENNETH: Ah, come on, Charlie, you got to bust loose every now and then. We'll have a couple of drinks.

EDDIE: (picks up phone) Mary, give me an outside line and don't give me no trouble. . . . Chickering 4-5099.

WALTER: Come on, Charlie, it's a short life, believe me.

Move in for CLOSEUP of Charlie, frowning. Over this, Eddie's voice.

EDDIE'S VOICE: Hello, hello, Louie? Is this Louie? . . . Louie, this is Eddie Watkins. I'd like to reserve a table for four for tonight. . . . For four . . .

CHARLIE: Hey, Eddie . . .

EDDIE'S VOICE: What?

CHARLIE: Count me in.

He immediately bends back to his work, takes his pencil up again. CAMERA PULLS QUICKLY UP AND AWAY until we have an ANGLE SHOT looking down at their desks in various positions of work.

EDDIE: (*on phone*) Louie, make that five. . . . Five guys . . . Yeah, a bachelor party . . .

FADE OUT

Poker & Cigars

Cigars and poker go together like bachelor parties and blow jobs. Don't forget cigars for the party. Nowadays they are almost as important as the booze and chicks. If you have a bunch of first-time smokers don't worry about getting expensive smokes. They won't know the difference.

—from *Great Bachelor Parties* by Herb Kavet

55

There is a long history

between the day Rodrigo de Jerez and Luís de Torres (Christopher Columbus's crewmen) stepped ashore in Cuba to take a few puffs of a tobacco wrapped in maize husks (the first Europeans to do so) and today's stag parties. Along the way the cigar has picked up lots of connotations: some power, a little vice, a certain entertainment caché (Cosby, George Burns, Groucho Marx) a touch of glamour, and last but not least the machismo thing. While cigar use peaked in 1964, its popularity surged again in the 1990s and it remains popular—especially among gatherings of men—today.

These tips come from the Oliva family, who started in Cuba in 1886 and now are the second-largest grower of Cuban-seed tobacco in Nicaragua. They oversee all aspects of their product, from seeds to smoking, and know a thing or two about fine cigars.

CIGAR SPEAK

CAP: A small piece of the wrapper that holds it in place
CROWN: The end you smoke
FOOT: The end you light
RING GAUGE: Girth of the cigar measured in 64ths of an inch
WRAPPER: The outside leaf of the cigar

SELECTING A CIGAR

First, decide the level of body you are comfortable with. Strength for the sake of strength is overrated. A full-body cigar should be felt in your stomach rather than in your throat or on your palate. The thickness of the wrapper leaf is a good measure of the body of a cigar. A thicker wrapper will generally deliver fuller body as it has a greater amount of oils. The thickness of the wrapper can be gauged by looking at the area where the wrapper overlaps in a cigar. Next, you will need to decide on a size. This should be determined by the amount of time you have available for smoking as well as the amount of smoke you enjoy. The large ring gauges (52–60) deliver large amounts of smoke and flavor. The medium ring gauges (43–50) are ideal for most blends as they are a good balance of smoke and flavor.

CUTTING A CIGAR

Several methods exist for cutting a cigar. It is generally a matter of personal preference. A scissor or guillotine cut usually provides a better draw. When cutting a cigar, special attention should be given not to cut below the "cap." The cap holds the wrapper in place, cutting below it can cause the wrapper to loosen. The crown of the cigar should be cut (test the draw then cut accordingly).

LIGHTING A CIGAR

When conditions allow, a cigar match is the preferred lighting source. However, the recent advances in the way of precision torch lighters have almost eclipsed the match. Either method is appropriate. Lighting a cigar properly requires one important note: Only apply fire to the exposed leaves at the end of the cigar. Do not burn the edges of the wrapper at the foot of the cigar. Roll the cigar and distribute the fire evenly. Once the exposed tobacco is evenly red your cigar is lit.

SMOKING A CIGAR

How one smokes a cigar will affect the overall flavor. Puffing quickly and often will raise the temperature of the cigar and result in a spicier smoke. You should take slow deliberate draws on the cigar, slowly releasing the smoke and enjoying the taste on your palate. Cigars should not be inhaled. The experience happens at the palate.

WHERE TO FIND THE BEST

BARCLAY-REX (75 Broad Street, New York, NY 10004; 212-962-3355; barclayrex.com) With four locations, they cater to all smokers from young to old, blue collar to Wall-Street suit, new smoker to experienced. Smoke and sip an espresso in the lounge at the Broad-Street location. DAVIDOFF OF GENEVA (davidoff.com) Dedicated to "the good life," including the love of beauty and elegance, of pleasure and living, Davidoff has been around since 1906. One of their first customers (after fleeing Kiev for Geneva) was Lenin. NAT SHERMAN (12 E. 42nd Street, New York, NY 10017; 800-MY-CIGAR or 212-764-5000; natsherman.com) When this family-owned company opened their shop in the 1930s they catered to fashion executives, show-business types and gangsters.

TOASTING & ROASTING

In ancient Greece, after-dinner drinking grew so rowdy that a chief overseer, called the symposiarch, became necessary. He not only managed the crowd but controlled the quantity of the liquor and the order of "healths" (or toasts) too. Today that job—along with the all-important task of setting the tone for the evening—goes to the best man. Cheers!

TOASTING 101

CUSTOMIZE Think of the crowd and tailor your toast appropriately.

PLAY THE FORTUNE-TELLER Tell a story about the groom that gives an idea of how he might react to married life or better yet how his spouse to be might react to living with him (mention something personal that she hasn't a clue about, like his fascination with MGM musicals). Don't forget to be good-natured about it.

COMPARE & CONTRAST Paint a picture of things his life is full of now and what they will be replaced with after marriage.

FINISH Make sure everyone knows the toast is over by saying "cheers" or "here's to your last days of freedom."

BYE–BYE BACHELORHOOD

"I propose a toast. Let us toast the good things in life. Freedom, irresponsibility, and young girls in bikinis. These are but some of the things you will be giving up, but we are sure you will be getting much in return. When you find out exactly what, be sure to let us know."

"A toast to us all. For tonight we lose another good man to the hungry beast of marriage and good sense. But it is not him for whom we should mourn. Oh no, he goes to a better place. It is we who that have to remain behind and drink the booze, chase the girls, go to the ball games, and party on into the night who must suffer. May we have the strength to endure this trial."

"Marriage is a romance in which the hero dies in the first chapter."

"Marriage is like a box of chocolates. You have to squeeze a few bottoms to make sure you like what you are getting."

Toasting & Roasting

"May your wife always fit you as your wedding ring—not too loose, not too tight, but just right!"

"Here's a toast to your new bride, who has everything a girl could want in her life, except for good taste in men!"

"Here's to King Solomon, ruler and sage,
The wisest of men in history's page
He had wives by the thousand, and thought it was fun . . .
Here's hoping you'll know how to handle just one."

"In olden times, sacrifices were made at the altar, a practice which is still very much practiced."

"Marriage is like a violin. After the music is over, you still have the strings."

"A toast to the groom. Although we gather tonight for a night of fun and teasing, we also remember the spark we see in our friend's eye when he is with his bride to be. We know the happiness that burns in him, and how he suffers when they are apart. To our friend and his coming marriage. Cheers!"

LOVE LINES

"Here's to love—the only fire against which there is no insurance."

"A man may kiss his wife goodbye,
The rose may kiss the butterfly,
The wine may kiss the frosted glass,
And you, my friends, may kiss my ass."

"Here's to the three rings of marriage!
The engagement ring, the wedding ring and the suffer-ring!"

"Here's to that which goes in hard and stiff
and comes out soft and wet.
Here's to . . . uh . . . bubblegum."

"Here's to the top
And here's to the middle
Let's hope tonight
We all get a little."

"A little sighing, a little crying, a little dying—
and a great deal of lying."

ON MERRYMAKING

"Here's to the men of all classes,
  Who through lasses and glasses
  Will make themselves asses!"

"O Lord God divine
  Who turned the water into wine
  Please forgive we foolish men
  We are going to turn it back again."

"Men soon tire of song and dances,
  Whiskey, gin and cheap romances,
  They want the finer things in life;
  A little home, and a charming wife,
  But they find joy in new caresses—
  So never lose those old addresses."

"Times are hard,
  And wages are small,
  So drink more beer,
  And fuck them all."

"Here's to all the kisses I've snatched . . .
  and vice versa!"

"Here's to the land we love!
  And here's to the love we land!"

"Here's to wives and sweethearts!
  May they never, never meet."

"Here's to a guy who is never blue,
  Here's to a buddy who is ever true,
  Here's to a pal, no matter what the load,
  Who never declines, just one for the road."

"Here's to the lasses we've loved, my lad,
  Here's to the lips we've pressed;
      For of kisses and lasses,
      Like liquor in glasses,
  The last is always the best."

INSULTS

"I would rather be with the people at this table
  than the finest people in the world!"

"Here's to you and your kind."

"Here's to good friends . . . and to you guys too!"

"Here's looking at you kid, though heaven knows
  it's an effort."

THE MARTINI
by Old Mr. Boston

Though the Martini is viewed with almost reverent awe as a drink of unique power, it is no more or less powerful than any other drink containing the same amount of alcohol.

The original Martini recipe called for one-half dry gin and one-half dry vermouth. This proportion began to change in the early 1940s to two or three parts dry gin to one part dry vermouth. Today, popular proportions for an extra-dry Martini range from a 5–to–1 to an 8–to–1 ratio. The greater the proportion of gin to vermouth, the "drier" the Martini.

ARE YOUR MARTINIS TOO STRONG?

Remember, America is nearly the only country in the world that drinks high-proof gin. The British, who perfected gin, and the Canadians prefer their gin at milder, smoother 80 proof. Today's very dry Martini can be returned to its original, more moderate proof only by using 80 proof gin.

MARTINI MIXING

Chill 3-ounce cocktail glasses to the point of frost. Fill Martini pitcher with cracked (not crushed) ice. Ice should be dry and hard frozen. Measure out the exact ingredients for the number of drinks required, pouring in the dry gin first (gin should "smoke" as it settles over the cold ice), then the dry vermouth. Stir briskly until drink is very cold. Strain at once into frosty, stemmed cocktail glasses. For Martinis "on the rocks," use pre-chilled Old-Fashioned glasses and pour the liquor over cubes of ice. A twist of lemon peel adds a special character to a Martini which many prefer.

MARTINI
(Traditional 2–to–1)
$1\frac{1}{2}$ oz. Old Mr. Boston dry gin
$\frac{3}{4}$ oz. dry vermouth
Serve with an olive

Drinking Games 1

Beer Hunter

Buzz level: Medium

Number of payers: 2 minimum

What's needed: A case of beer and nerves of steel

The rules are so easy, a drunkard could understand them. All you need for this game is a good supply of canned beer and a box.

Take several cans and shake them. (The number of cans you select will add to the tension). Now I don't mean just shake them, I mean SHAKE 'EM till they are about to blow up. Then put them in the box with the others and mix them around (one person not looking) and then switch them around again (a second person not looking). So nobody knows where they are.

Now, one person picks a can, holds it to their head at an angle, and opens it. If it's not a shaken one, they have to drink it all in one go. If it is one of the shaken cans, everyone will know it! Keep going around the room until all the cans have been drunk or exploded. Repeat as necessary.

Beat the Bartender

Buzz level: Extremely high

Number of payers: 1 plus audience

What's needed: Money, balls

Another game for the insane, with a very high buzz factor. As the story goes, nobody has ever won, lost or drawn.

Some tips: Don't play it in a crowded bar (you may lose track of your bartender); make sure the bar staff are friendly and can take a joke (very important to avoid a draw); don't make any plans for the following morning.

How to play: 1. The drinker approaches the bar and orders a shot drink (whisky, bourbon, vodka). 2. The drinker pays for the drink with too much money (i.e., hands over $5 for a $2 shot.) 3. As the bartender goes away to get change, the drinker shoots the shot. 4. When the bartender returns with the change, go to step number 1.

The game is scored or ends in a number of possible ways: Drinker falls over (Result: Bar wins); bartender punches drinker's lights out (Result: Draw); Drinker gets thrown out (Result: Draw); Bar closes (Result: Drinker wins).

STAGS ON FILM

CAPTAIN KIDD'S KIDS (1919) Hal Roach (of *Our Gang* aka "Little Rascals" fame) directs Harold Lloyd through a series of wild adventures including, but not limited to, female pirates.

BACHELOR APARTMENTS (1920) Our hero, I. O. Underwood, realizes that he must either go to work or marry. Through a series of mix-ups—and a bit of drink at a bachelor dinner—he ends up with two girls.

THE ACE OF CADS (1926) Two officers in the British Guards fall for the same girl. One loses his fiancée, but all is not lost.

THE BODY DISAPPEARS (1941) Sci-fi meets screwball comedy when millionaire Peter DeHaven passes out at his bachelor party and wakes up the victim of a prank gone terribly wrong (involving the morgue and an eccentric professor).

THE BACHELOR PARTY (1957) Paddy Chayefsky's tale of working-class despair unfolds at bookkeeper Charlie Samson's bachelor party. Carolyn Jones plays the crazy Greenwich Village party girl.

HOW TO MURDER YOUR WIFE (1965) Jack Lemon, successful cartoonist and con-firmed bachelor, falls in love with the girl in the cake at a friend's bachelor do and almost spontaneously marries her. The next day he has second thoughts. Craziness ensues.

THE ECSTASIES OF WOMEN (1969) During a night-long bachelor party Harry reminisces with the go-go dancer about his many conquests.

BACHELOR PARTY (1984) This Tom Hanks classic involves a wealthy bride to be (and her friends) dressing as prostitutes in order to sneak in to bus driver Hanks' bach-elor party to keep an eye on him.

DATE WITH AN ANGEL (1987) A sexy-but-silent angel falls into the swimming pool of a bachelor who's hung over from his bach-elor party. Phoebe Cates stars as the fiancée who can't understand what's happening.

NINJA BACHELOR PARTY (1991) This low-budget martial-arts parody follows Clarence Mumford, a Robitussin addict living with his parents, on his quest to become a ninja master.

THE NIGHT THAT NEVER HAPPENED (1997) A secret pact binds all those attending a spontaneous bachelor party that eventually involves the usual—strippers, drinking—along with a host of other he-man adventures like kidnapping, blackmail, and grand theft.

STAG (1997) This made-for-TV movie stars Mario Van Peebles and John Stockwell as successful men who throw a booze-drugs-and-strippers bachelor party, but all ends in tears after an accidental killing.

VERY BAD THINGS (1998) This black comedy involving a bachelor party going very wrong is quite similar in plot to *Stag*—only better. It stars Jon Favreau, Cameron Diaz, Jeremy Piven and Christian Slater.

BACHELOR PARTY OVEREXPOSED (2001) A wild and crazy bachelor party does no favors for couple Ameere (Mike Davis) and Jacquelyne's (Shawn Schaffer) struggling relationship.

WORLD'S WILDEST BACHELOR PARTIES (2002) This edition of the World's Wildest series (Bar Fights, Chick Fights, Deathmatches and College Parties, among others) features all the bad-boy stunts a bachelor party could possibly entail.

A GUY THING (2003) A week before his wedding, Paul (Jason Lee) meets a grass-skirt-wearing tiki dancer named Becky (Julia Stiles) at his bachelor winding and wakes up in bed with her the next day. A kooky cover-up is concocted when Becky shows up at a pre-wedding family get-together.

AMERICAN WEDDING (2003) All your favorite characters from *American Pie* reappear for Jim's (Jason Biggs) wedding, and the secret bachelor party is just one obstacle on the way to the altar.

SIDEWAYS (2004) One of the more sober (so to speak) films in the "bachelor party" genre, this film follows sort-of pathetic best friends Miles (Paul Giamatti) and Jack

(Thomas Haden Church) on a touching if awkward road trip through California's wine country before Jack marries.

WILLIE D: BACHELOR PARTY—RAW & EXPOSED (2004) Hip-hop artist Willie D (of the notorious horror-rap group Geto Boys) and his entourage take you on a wild ride through Houston's wildest clubs before he ties the knot.

BACHELOR PARTY LAS VEGAS (2006) A group of friends head to Vegas to throw their best friend the best bachelor party ever.

BACHELOR PARTY MASSACRE (2006) The title pretty much sums up the plot, which involves a secluded summer retreat, strippers and—what a mistake!—a psychotic blonde serial killer incorrectly thought to be "the entertainment."

BACHELOR PARTY 2: THE LAST TEMPTATION (2007) The 24-years-later "sequel" to Tom Hanks' *Bachelor Party* is more like a remake. There is an out-of-control bachelor party with drinks and bikini-clad women and nasty in-laws.

STAGKNIGHT (2007) A story about a paintball outing gone bad—very, very bad. This slasher-like film takes place in the deep dark forest outside London, where, unbeknownst to the "Weekend Warriors," an ancient evil has lain undisturbed for centuries.

MEXICAN SUNRISE (2007) Based on a true story about a group of guys who threw a bachelor shindig south of the border—not all of whom made it back. Tense and edgy, this film, told in a series of flashbacks and flash-forwards, keeps you guessing until the end.

71

Office Strip

If you know the groom from a business setting you can have a great start to a bachelor party by bringing the stripper to a business meeting. Introduce her as a new computer analyst and have her begin with a business presentation then start her routine in the conference room. Remember to close the door.

—from *Great Bachelor Parties*
by Herb Kavet

73

STAG PRANKS

A great bachelor party or stag night wouldn't be complete without a once-in-a-lifetime prank that delights and can be retold for years to come. And yet the tricky part is that this stunt should also—if all goes well—leave the bachelor alive, un-maimed and with his self-esteem relatively intact. The key to success seems to involve a clever combination of creativity and humiliation. Here are a few classic capers to get the wheels turning.

CALL YOURSELF A TRANNY?

1. Pour drinks down the groom's gullet until he passes out.
2. Put him back in his room.
3. Remove all his personal effects (and all bedding).
4. Leave his travel documents (tickets/passport/ etc.) in the room.
5. Place a dress of choice (a mini is always nice; undergarments optional) and matching shoes by the travel documents.
6. Return home and wait for him.

ADAM & STEVE

1. Arrange for the groom to be treated to an onstage lap dance.
2. Have the stripper hand-cuff him to a pole.
3. Have the stripper pay special attention by rubbing oil into his chest, etc.
4. Have the stripper reveal that she's really a he.

BACKDRAFT

1. Distract the groom.
2. Take his suitcase and remove all his pants.
3. Place a pair of pants with the cheeks cut out into the suitcase along with a frilly pair of underwear.

SMURF SHINDIG

1. Hire a dwarf and paint him blue and costume him like a Smurf.
2. Handcuff him to the stag for the entire weekend. (*see page 99*)

"I once helped shrink wrap my brother to a lamp post . . . then put a sign on him that read, "Have a go . . . $1 each."

OTHER PRANKISH DARES!

- Dare him to wear a dress to every bar and ask the first man he sees if he comes here often.
- Strip your stag, face him toward a lamppost with his arms around it and shrink wrap everything except his ass.
- On the way to or from a club, stop the car a good 3 to 5 miles away. Strip him and give him the choice: shoes or shorts. If he chooses shorts, tear them off, give him 5 dollars an tell him he's got 30 minutes to get to the destination where his clothes will be given back (extra points for giving him a man-size diaper or giant underwear upon arrival instead).

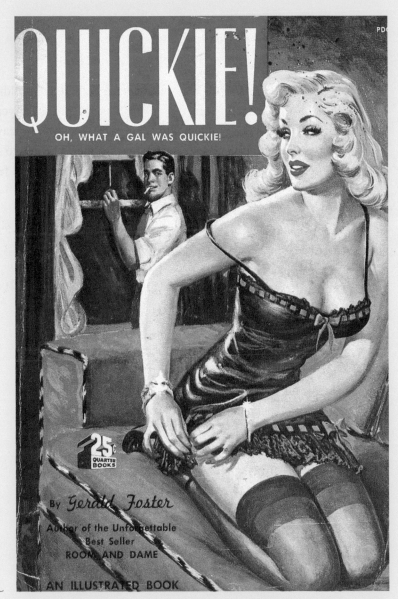

ACTIVITY

MAKE A SIMPLE BALL AND CHAIN

In pirate days a ball and chain was fairly easy to come by. Today, however, the best way to get this classic bachelor-party favorite is to make it yourself.

MATERIALS

Bowling ball
(12 to 16 pounds is ideal, but use your discretion)

Epoxy adhesive
(the strongest you can find, or any glue your hardware store says will hold a chain inside a 12-to-16-pound bowling ball's finger hole)

Chain
(links sized to fit into a bowling ball's finger hole and long enough so the groom can carry it while walking)

Padlock and key

Metallic Sharpie pen or paint

Black spray paint
(depending on the color of your bowling ball)

INSTRUCTIONS

1. Spray paint the bowling ball black (if it's not black already). Let dry.

2. Scrape the inside of the largest finger hole in the bowling ball (in order to help the glue stick better).

3. Fill the scraped-up finger hole with the glue, following instructions, and place one end of the chain in the glue. Let completely dry (this can take several days).

4. Use a silver or gold Sharpie or silver or gold paint and write the fiancée's name on the ball, or, if you are more artistic, doodle a caricature.

HOW TO USE

When the time is right, wrap the end of the chain around the groom's leg and padlock it securely.

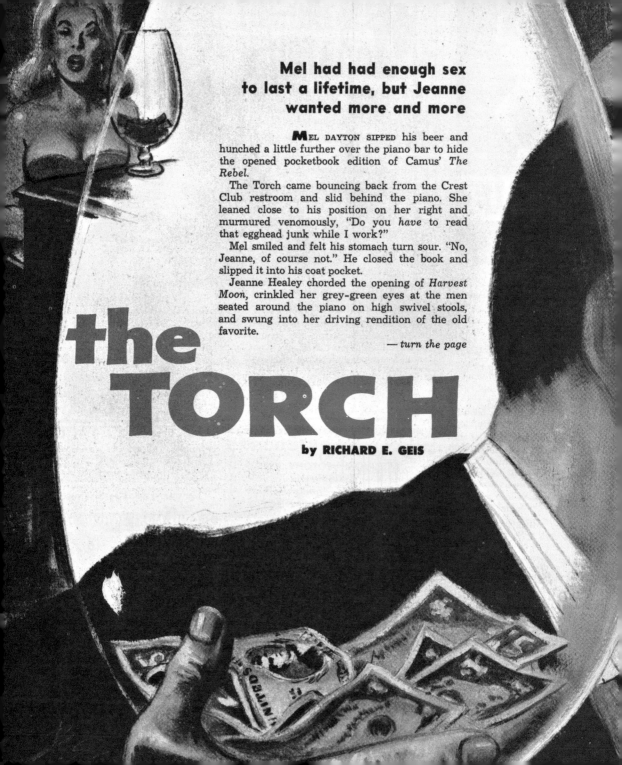

**Mel had had enough sex
to last a lifetime, but Jeanne
wanted more and more**

Mel Dayton sipped his beer and
hunched a little further over the piano bar to hide
the opened pocketbook edition of Camus' *The
Rebel.*

The Torch came bouncing back from the Crest
Club restroom and slid behind the piano. She
leaned close to his position on her right and
murmured venomously, "Do you *have* to read
that egghead junk while I work?"

Mel smiled and felt his stomach turn sour. "No,
Jeanne, of course not." He closed the book and
slipped it into his coat pocket.

Jeanne Healey chorded the opening of *Harvest
Moon*, crinkled her grey-green eyes at the men
seated around the piano on high swivel stools,
and swung into her driving rendition of the old
favorite.

— turn the page

the TORCH

by RICHARD E. GEIS

Dirty Ditties

Cup Cakes

by Terri "Cup Cake" O'Mason

Spoken Introduction: I've read so many articles about the way to a man's heart being through his tummy that I decided to take a few cooking lessons. A couple of weeks ago I asked my boyfriend home for dinner. I fixed a nice steak, and I made some biscuits, baked a cake and a pie. But he didn't seem very impressed with it all, and it sort of hurt my feelings until after dinner I found out that . . . uhhh. . .

He liked to nibble on my cupcakes,
He just went nuts about their taste,
They seemed to melt right in his mouth,
    I've never had complainers
They're smooth as silk, they're filled with milk
And he said they come in such cute . . . containers.

Oh you should see my lovely cupcakes,
They are much too nice to go to waste,
I asked him if he'd like a bite,
And now he bites 'em every night.
He likes to nibble on my cupcakes.

He likes to nibble on my cupcakes,
Just like his mother's they're just right . . . and left,
They're not too big, they're not too small,
They fit right in his grip
They're not too hard and not too soft,
And there's a raisin on each . . . tip.

Oh you should see my lovely cupcakes,
They made him raise a hearty appetite,
They're juicier than any steak,
And he found out that they weren't fake
He likes to nibble on my cupcakes

       Man this guy is always eatin'.

Stag party

A TOTAL-RANGE
HIGH FIDELITY
RECORDING

DOOTO

Allen
Drew

Slightly Naughty
JOKES!

Two lobbyists met at a party in Washington. "How's business?" one asked the other.

"Well, you know how it is," said the other. "This business is like sex. When it's good it's wonderful. When it's bad—it's still pretty good."

I warned my sister not to marry a lawyer. I told her all he liked to do was talk, talk, talk! But she wouldn't listen to me. However, I must say my sister's not afraid to admit she made a mistake. She told me that all her husband did during their honeymoon was jabber, jabber, jabber.

I'D ASK YOU IN... BUT I DON'T KNOW WHAT FOR—NOW!

It was New Year's Eve, and the house was brightly decorated with sprigs of holly and mistletoe. Only the clicking of Grandma's knitting needles broke the silence. The children, Polly, eight, and Janice, six, were seated before the roaring fireplace leafing through a picture book. They rose and went over to Grandma's rocker. Polly climbed up on the arm of the chair, and Janice snuggled into Grandma's warm lap.

"Tell us a story, Grandma," Janice pleaded.

"Oh," said the old lady putting aside her knitting and wrapping her arms about the children, "what should I tell you about?"

Little Polly's voice came gently.

"Tell us about the time you were a whore in Chicago."

A pretty young thing bicycled from one end of town to the other over the roughest cobblestone streets. "My," she said, "I'll never come that way again."

One day during an ancient war, a tall, strong, and handsome Roman soldier broke into a house where he found two luscious maidens and their matronly nurse.

Chuckling with glee, he roared, "Prepare thyselves for a conquest, my pretties."

The lovely girls fell to their knees and pleaded with him. "Do with us as thou wilt, O Roman, but spare our faithful old nurse."

"Shut thy mouth," snapped the nurse. "War is war."

George was trying to convince his buddy Hank that the new working girl in town was better than any of her predecessors. "I tell you, Hank, this girl is as good as my own wife."

"That so?" Hank asked. "All right. Let's go over there."

So they went to see the new girl, and they paid for a visit. On the way out George asked Hank for his opinion.

"Well," he said, "she's good, all right, but not as good as your wife."

He: "Do you like cocktails?"
She: "Why yes, tell one."

" *THAT REMINDS ME...
I HAVE A DATE WITH
DICK TO-NITE !* "

We know a cutie who says she has sex insomnia—she just can't keep her thighs closed.

At an isolated part of the beach at Cannes, a beautiful French girl threw herself into the sea. A young man off at a distance noticed it and dashed into the water to save her, but it was too late. He dragged the semi-nude body ashore and left it on the sand while he went in search of some official. When he returned, he was horrified to see a man making love to the corpse.

"*Monsieur!*" he exclaimed. "That woman is dead!"

"*Sacre Bleu!*" muttered the man, jumping up. "I thought she was an American."

Drinking Games 2

Beer Bungee

Buzz level: Low to medium, but the laugh level can be quite high

Number of Players: 2 and up

What's needed: Beer (in a large mug for best splash results, but cans or bottles will do), beer decoys, 10 to 20 feet of bungee cord (or some stretchy device of your own making like inner tubes linked together to form a chain)

Perhaps a little less intrepid than stepping off a bridge into the abyss with only one thin string between you and certain death, this game does, however, offer the possibility of a lot more laughs and will quench your thirst at the same time.

How to play: 1. Attach the bungee cord securely to a tree or wall at about waist height. 2. Set up the real beer and the decoys on a bar or table just beyond the reach of the cord. 3. Choose the playing order (let the groom go first, followed by anyone who's actually bungee jumped). 4. When the player is attached to the cord someone yell "start" and everyone then counts out the time it takes the player to reach and drink a beer.

Scoring: Take the time counted by the crowd and add five seconds for grabbing a decoy and five seconds for spilling more than half the beer. Lowest score wins.

Drop the Dime

Buzz level: Medium-high

Number of players: 2 and up

What's needed: A cigarette, a napkin, a dime, a glass and a rubber band or some tape to hold the napkin over the mouth of the glass

What better way to combine drinking and smoking than playing Drop the Dime? This more-macho form of the popular kids' game Don't Break the Ice will have the party hopping in no time.

How to play: 1. Stretch the napkin over the top of the glass and secure it with tape or a rubber band. 2. Place the dime on top of the napkin. 3. Each player takes his turn holding the lit cigarette in his mouth and making a single hole in the napkin. Whoever causes the dime to drop into the glass has to drink a full pint of beer.

Cheater's hint: blowing lightly (and surreptitiously) on your opponent's cigarette may help speed the burn.

I USED TO BE ABLE TO HOLD MY LIQUOR!

The Girls of Greenwich Village

by Peter Eldridge

Such are the attractions of Susan March (her lifework is photographing bearded men in New York's Greenwich Village) that to view her in profile might be to miss seeing the expensive 35-millimeter camera (with telescopic lens) that is at all times suspended from the classic ivory column of her neck.

Susan is a corn-fed Iowa blond who arrived in New York two years ago, when she was 19. She's a good photographer. And she works in any available light. Living simply, she spends what money she makes on photo gadgets, and camera fans who have come upon Susan in the Village are astounded by her remarkable equipment.

In Podunk, Peoria, or Poseyville, Indiana, a young woman such as Susan might be hauled before the city fathers and required to explain exactly what it is that makes her so much a wizard in the darkroom that men are her most willing subjects.

But not so in New York's Greenwich Village. In Greenwich Village, Susan March is only one of 4,000 young women of various gifts and talents who have voluntarily broken away from the bonds of convention, the better to serve in the shrine of the lively arts.

Even the most nearsighted of men should be able to look at this setup and recognize a good thing when he sees it. For, in lower Manhattan, there is an incredible plenty of meat and drink for every taste and thirst.

Nothing quite describes this galaxy of girls in Greenwich Village as well as does this verse, which the late Maxwell Bodenheim once sold to me in the Minetta Tavern for the price of a gin-and-beer cement mixer.

A miraculous feast of maidens,
Like that of the loaves
*   and the fishes,*
Where nobody lays the table,
And nobody washes the dishes

Bodenheim's particular poetic license allowed him a certain artistic freewheeling, for it must be admitted that not *every* one

The Girls of Greenwich Village

of the 4,000 young ladies in Greenwich Village is always and instantly available. Still, there is no argument with the fact that the presence of a full regiment of so-called emancipated women in a single residential district of New York City is an extraordinary circumstance. The girls are there, all right. But how come? What lodestone attracts them to this area? Where do they hail from? What are their backgrounds? What do these lovely daubers and dabblers and do-it-yourselfers honestly hope to find? And what *do* they find?

The truth is that most of these young ladies have come to Greenwich Village in search of will-o'-the-wisp which nobody has ever really seen. They arrive from the four corners of the United States—from Denver, Danville, and Duluth; from Boston, Beaumont, and the Bronx.

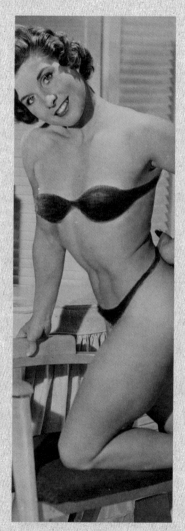

A few of the girls come to work hard and earnestly at their respective arts and crafts. But most come as renegades, others as refugees from "middle class conformity." And still others swarm to the old hives like recruits for some unnamed, new world order. Once arrived, they hang Chilean copper from their ears and necks, they bind their bodies in bootstained-leather jerkins, and they gird their waists with rawhide belts and bands of beaten brass. This year's uniform consists of skintight frontier pants, black cotton stockings, and loden-cloth car coats. Only a few of them use makeup. Theirs is the cult of looking too careless to be successful and too indifferent to be failures.

Because the gaff is hard to stand, the turnover is terrific. The majority of these free-thinking hopefuls last from three months to a year. Those who are partially subsidized by money from home sometimes last a little longer. In the end, most of them give up gracefully, go back to where they came from, or try to find jobs in Macy's. But the Village still magnetizes others, for once upon a time, studio rents were cheap and the pushcarts on Mulberry Street offered a variety of ten-cent meals which might be simmered into savory feasts—provided the sculptor down the hall contributed a box of spaghettini. Today, when groceries run low, there is always some uptowner on the make, a working stiff who is good for a gutstuffing of veal parmigiani at Fugazy's on Saturday night. And if the landlady threatens to saw off the key in the lock on Thursday morning, the rent party on Wednesday eve manages to assemble the needed cash.

You hear about rent parties along the bar in San Remo's, or in the men's room at Louis' on Sheridan Square. If you're desperate to find one, just look to see who buys "four to go" at Frank's Pizzeria on Bleecker Street, or follow where the O'Sullivan points his beard as he lopes along Morton Street, lugging his guitar. He'll lead you to the doin's.

The rent party itself is quite a ball. The hostess and a muscleman are posted at the door. Drop a dollar into the taped-up cigar box and you're in. You peer through the smoke, guard your eardrums against the hi-fi, and sniff the savor of pizza and social significance. There is always a female "my parents don't understand me" soul to massage. Sad to say, too many of them, and a man would do well to avoid them: These are the vestal virgins in the temple

of the arts and they would rather walk a gentleman past some famous poet's house on Patchin Place than lead a man astray. Also, this kind of woman usually eats like a matched team of percherons.

Should a man prefer a horse of a slightly different color, he has only to walk into the Riviera and elbow his way to the bar. In the Riviera, across the street from Louis' on Sheridan Square, his luck is sure to change.

The darker-skinned peoples hold forth at the Riviera, and with them, the color line is never drawn. If you play it right, you might get to meet Ayesha Dauphine leaning her remarkable rib cage against the bar. She claims to be an Arab and there is no doubt that she has memorized a verse or two from the Koran. But she has a fund of still more vital knowledge which never came

Keep your eyes wide open before marriage, and half shut afterwards.

—Benjamin Franklin

out of a book. In the planes of her face there is the suggestion of docility, a hint of the do-what-you-wish-to-me much to be desired in a harem slave. The planes of her body are unbelievably sinuous. When Ayesha talks, she whispers and lets you see her teeth and the tip of her serpentlike tongue. She leans too close. But that's Ayesha.

The size of an evening in Greenwich Village is usually dependent upon the mood of the hunter. For example, a safari to the ordinary waterholes sometimes flushes an extraordinary bird of passage. And there is no indication in the cards that you will encounter only intellectual wildebeest and eye-glassed hippopotami at the Eighth Street Book Store or the galleries on Tenth Street.

Directing one's chukka boots across the Avenue of the Ameri-cas, past craft studios, gourmet shops, and a string of espresso houses, you'll reach the book stalls which feature "arty" paperbacks and remaindered hardcover specials. You might also find yourself standing next to Maynell Talbot, a pale poet from Perdido, Alabama, who, by her own admission, has paused in Greenwich Village on her way to hell.

Maynell has ash blonde hair, mild blue eyes, and a 39-inch bust. She can't keep her cotton pickin' hands off art-bound copies of Proust and Christopher Isherwood. She writes the best of her poetry in bed, dictating into the microphone of a tape recorder.

"Ah want to be Olympian and look down on life," Maynell told me. "When they's all this misery and sufferin' in this world, it's the only possible point of view."

A 39-inch bust can be distracting. "Yes," I agreed with her. "It's best to be above these things." And I sure wasn't whistling Dixie.

With 4,000 freedom-happy women encamped between 14th Street and Jones Alley, it is only natural that one runs into the good and the bad, the sweet and the tart. For example, there are wholesome types who are as frank and as open as the prairies. But there are also the hard-eyed "we're against *people!*" misses in britches. There are short ones, tall ones, fat ones and skinny ones, and to avoid confusion we have compiled a kind of guide for men who just might not know where to look first.

Although the average man's night is the Greenwich Villager's day, the opposite is not necessarily true. An afternoon's walk in the right direction need not be solely for the purpose of exercise. Hard by the graceful arch that marks the Fifth Avenue entrance to Washington Square Park is a shallow pigeon-spattered fountain. Congregated here, you will find a number of young men and women in fine fettle and paint-daubed dungarees. Beneath dirty sweatshirts beat hearts that are free, and the throats under the bright paisley shawls swell to the strains of folk songs and calypso chants. If you bring your own guitar, you can work up a clique of your own. If not, you could do worse than to memorize the last three choruses of "Joe Hill." There is nothing like close harmony for getting a man past the fringes of a daisy chain and into the charmed circle.

If you can't fry fat at the fountain, walk south to Sheridan Square, and look through the plate-glass partitions of Joe

Atkins Food Shop. Surely you will find something which appeals to *your* taste! If you can make conversation, you should have very little trouble making time.

If you're new at this sort of thing and are afraid of locking horns with an old hand at the game, go to Gay Street (that's its *real* name, bub!). At number 14, you will find the site of the fabled cellar apartment which was the tender trap in *My Sister Eileen*. For some extraordinary reason, number 14 is a kind of shrine for the new arrivals from West of the Mississippi. You are sure to run into a good-looking gawper with *pressed* frontier pants, which is the most flagrant of all tip-offs. Westerners are notoriously friendly, so, if you still need help at this point, you're not worth being taken in hand. But we'll do it, anyway. 🎴

93

Drinking Games 3

Fuzzy Duck

Buzz level: Low

Number of players: At least four, but the more the merrier

What's needed: Drinks and a penchant for tongue twisting

How to play: 1. Assemble everyone in a circle (or around a table) with their drinks at hand. 2. The groom starts by saying "fuzzy duck" to the guy on his left. 3. That guy continues by saying "fuzzy duck" to the guy on his left and so on around the group. 4. The game continues like this until someone decides to change the direction by saying "does he?" (or "duzzie?"). 5. Now, not only does the game change direction (going rightward), but the phrase changes to "ducky fuzz." 6. The direction and phrase continue like that until someone says the magic word "duzzie?" again, at which point the phrase goes back to "fuzzy duck" and the direction goes left.

How to lose: Anyone who makes a mistake takes a drink.

Xtreme Fuzzy Duck: Play as above adding the rule that each player cannot say the same phrase (either "fuzzy duck" or "ducky fuzz") twice in a row. In other words, if it comes his turn to speak and he said "fuzzy duck" last time, he cannot say it again. He must either change direction by saying "duzzie?" or he can say "ducky fuzz" if the direction has already been changed before coming back to him.

"Hi Bob"

Buzz level: Medium-high

Number of players: Unlimited

What's needed: DVD player, DVDs of *The Bob Newhart Show*, beer

This mellow game is for diehard beer-drinking Bob Newhart fans, and can surprisingly get a buzz on quick.

How to play: 1. Turn on the DVD and play an episode of *The Bob Newhart Show*. 2. Every time someone says "Hi Bob," everyone takes a drink.

How to win: there are no winners or losers in the end, only tipsy Bob Newhart fans.

Variations: Substitute *I Love Lucy* and "Luuuucy," *24* and Jack Bauer saying "Dammit," *Cheers* and every time Norm touches his beer. . . you get the idea.

DON'T JUST STAND THERE, MAN,
TAKE OFF THE COAT AND JOIN THE PARTY!

Dirty Ditties

Have a Good Time

by Terri "Cup Cake" O'Mason

Have a good time when you're in your prime,
'Cause it don't mean a thing when you're old,
Take a chance on romance, 'cause what can you lose?
Later on boys you're gonna blow out a fuse.

Go out and make hay while you're feeling okay,
Don't be like a fellow that I know,
He went up to a lake and rented a canoe,
His girl was 18, he was 82,
He paddled and paddled, what else could he do?

You better take my advice, 'cause listen here Jack,
Once you squeeze that toothpaste out you can't put it back,
Go out and make love under stars above,
Get a little fun out of life.

Sure, gals like guys with money, I admit it's true,
But any guy can be popular if he knows a thing or two,
Why don't you do to her what you try to get her to do to you,
And you'll both have a wonderful time.

Be just like a sailor, have a girl in every port,
All a female expects of a man is to be a good sport,
And if you want some new tricks, read that Kinsey Report,
That'll never be out of date.

I'll take my marriage serious, it'll pay dividends,
I won't be too blasé, 'cause that's where marriage ends,
And I'll never sleep with strangers, only with his best friends,
And we'll all have a wonderful time.

And he's got more friends!

RENT-A-LITTLE FUN*
A Idea not Short on Laughs

"**Across the nation,** little people are being hired as party greeters, ring bearers, bartenders (who stand on the bar), tribute bands, celebrity impersonators and entertainers. They've even been hired to show up at corporate events as mini-CEOs," says the *Los Angeles Times*.

For bachelor parties, however, little people/dwarfs are mostly hired to box, strip, dance with strippers, just mingle or, as one report has it, to be painted as a Smurf and handcuffed to the groom (see below). Perhaps your groom will be impressed if leprechauns, Oompa Loompas or the Lollipop Kid show up at his do. That depends on his personality and interests. Whatever your motivation, if you're considering dwarfs as entertainment, you are already thinking creatively, and there is no doubt that a little person or two can bring a whole new dimension to your Stag Night party.

A Short List of Where To Find Little People

ShortEntertainment.biz
HireLittlePeople.com
TinyEntertainment.com
DwarfEntertainment.com

TALL TALE OR URBAN MYTH?

It's been widely reported on the internet that a group of English lads hired a dwarf, painted him blue, dressed him like a Smurf, brought him to a foreign country and handcuffed him to the bachelor for the entire four-day bachelor celebration. Let's hope the "Smurf," who was literally attached to the bridegroom throughout the long weekend—eating, drinking, sleeping, and showering (among others things) with him—didn't ruin him for the bride-to-be.

*According to Little People of America (lpaonline.net) the word "midget" is considered offensive—a throwback to circus days and used by the ignorant. Better to say "little person," "dwarf," or "short-statured" instead.

MANLY MENUS

Four Quick & Easy Bachelor Bash Menus

FOR THE HE-MAN

TO DRINK: *Beer & Wine* STARTER: *Red and Yellow Beefsteak Tomato Salad* MAIN: *Fire up the barbie for Steaks, Ribs, Salmon Steaks & Vegetables* DESSERT: *Spiked Watermelon*

BEST STEAKS FOR GRILLING: Going to the butcher is a good idea, especially if he has USDA Prime Aged steak (not so common, but the best). Otherwise you want Choice rib-eye, porterhouse, T-bone or tenderloin from $1^1/_2$ to 3 inches thick. Being well-marbled is the key, because it stands up best to the high heat of the grill. Keep seasoning simple: salt and pepper, maybe a little garlic. Do not ever poke the steak with a fork. Allow the juices to remain inside until served. To test for doneness use your thumb or the palm of your hand: spongy for rare, some resistance for medium, firm when well-done.

SPIKED WATERMELON
Serves at least 8 people

Watermelon (10 lbs. or larger, with seeds
　for spitting contest after)
1 bottle (750 ml) chilled vodka (no flavors!)

1. Cut a plug about 3 inches deep and as wide as the bottle neck (try tracing the bottle cap with a sharpie) out of the watermelon. Save the plug. **2.** Stick the bottleneck in the hole and let the vodka drain into the watermelon (figure about $1/_2$ to 1 cup absorption per hour). **3.** Re-plug the watermelon and refrigerate overnight. **4.** Serve chilled with the bottle sticking out of the melon.

Variation: Remove about $1/_4$ cup vodka from bottle (take a shot), mix $1/_4$ cup sugar and juice of two lemons until dissolved, then add to vodka along with 2 mint sprigs. Let sit overnight, then use as above.

FOR THE URBAN HIPSTER (BRUNCH)

TO DRINK: *Champagne, Champagne Punch or Champagne Drinks*
STARTER: *Quinoa & Whole Wheat Pancakes* MAIN: *Quiche (or Lobster Omelets)*
DESSERT: *Selection of Dark Chocolates & Sparkling Dessert Wine*

QUINOA & WHOLE WHEAT PANCAKES
Makes about 8 pancakes

$1/3$ cup quinoa flour
$1/3$ cup whole wheat pastry flour
$1/3$ cup unbleached white flour
$1/2$ teaspoon salt
$1/2$ teaspoon baking soda
1 teaspoon baking powder
1 egg
3 tablespoons oil
$1/3$ cup yogurt
$2/3$ cup soy milk

1. Stir all dry ingredients together. **2.** Beat all wet ingredients together. **3.** Mix liquid ingredients into dry and allow to stand for 5 minutes.
4. Meanwhile, heat griddle or skillet over medium heat until a drop of water sizzles. **5.** Pour batter over griddle (about $1/4$ cup per pancake). When bubbles burst, flip. Cook until golden brown.
6. Serve with real maple syrup.

Macho, schmacho! This quiche is easy to make, tastes great and serves a crowd. Add to or subtract from the filling at whim.

QUICHE
Yields one 9-inch quiche

BATTER: *3 eggs*
2 egg yolks
2 cups heavy cream
2 tablespoons flour
Salt and pepper

FILLING:
At least 1 cup grated Gruyère cheese, chopped ham, sautéed onions, chopped broccoli

1. Preheat oven to 375°F. **2.** Beat batter ingredients. **3.** Cover an unbaked 9-inch pie shell with the grated cheese. **4.** Add ham, onions and chopped broccoli and pour batter over filling. **5.** Bake for at least 30 minutes or until puffy and firm.

FOR THE GEEK

TO DRINK: Romulan Ale with Tetris Ice Cubes or Klingon Martinis
STARTER: Genetically Modified Veggies & Onion Dip MAIN: Ultimate Macaroni & Cheese
DESSERT: Yoda Cookies or D&D Dragon Cake

ROMULAN ALE (Commanders' Grade)

1 fifth Blue Curaçao, 1 pint Smirnoff 100 vodka; 6 oz. Amaretto di Saronno, 6 oz. sweet vermouth, 3 oz. Midori or melon liqueur

KLINGON MARTINI

One part gin, one part vermouth, a dash of bloodwine.
Serve in a traditional martini glass without the olive.

ULTIMATE MACARONI & CHEESE
Makes 6 servings

Choose a medium-sized pasta with grooves, twists and/or curves that will hold a maximum of the cheese sauce. Varieties such as macaroni, gemelli, radiatore, rotini, shells or fusilli are ideal. You can skip the onion/bay leaf/peppercorn infusion for the béchamel sauce to save time; it adds a subtle layer of savory flavor to the dish.

2¹/₂ cups (9 ounces) dry pasta
2¹/₂ cups whole milk
1 slice onion
1 bay leaf

10 whole black peppercorns
4 tablespoons unsalted butter
¹/₄ cup all-purpose flour
8 oz. sharp cheddar cheese, grated (about 2¹/₂ cups)
3 oz. fontina cheese, grated (about 1 cup)
3 oz. Emmenthal, Gruyère or similar Swiss-type cheese, grated (about 1 cup)
Salt and freshly ground black pepper
¹/₂ cup fresh bread crumbs

1. Preheat the oven to 350°F. Generously butter a 2-quart baking dish. **2.** Bring a large pot of salted water to a boil. Stir in the pasta

I've been in love with the
same woman for forty-one
years. If my wife finds
out, she'll kill me!

—Henny Youngman

and boil until it is about half cooked, tender on the surface with a distinct bite still in the center, about 5 minutes. Drain well, rinse with cold water and set aside, tossing from time to time as it cools to avoid sticking. **3.** Put the milk in a small saucepan with the onion slice, bay leaf and peppercorns. Bring just to a low boil over medium heat, then take the pan from the heat and let sit to infuse for 10 to 15 minutes. (If skipping the aromatics, simply warm the milk.) **4.** Melt the butter in a large saucepan over medium heat. Whisk in the flour and cook, whisking constantly, until it foams up and has a very slight toasty smell (it should not brown), 1 to 2 minutes. Strain the warm milk into the pan and whisk to blend. Continue to cook the sauce, whisking often, until it thickens, about 5 minutes. Turn off the heat and gradually whisk in the cheeses until fully melted. Season the sauce to taste with salt and pepper, then add the pasta and stir to fully coat all the pasta with the cheese sauce. **5.** Pour the mixture into the prepared dish and sprinkle the bread crumbs evenly over. Set the dish on the oven rack and lay a piece of foil on the rack below to catch any drips. Bake until the macaroni and cheese is bubbling hot and the top is nicely browned, about 40 minutes. Let sit for about 15 minutes before serving.

FOR THE SECOND (OR MORE) MARRIAGE

TO DRINK: Pitchers of Margaritas or Mexican Beer STARTER: Guacamole
MAIN: Mexican Beer Chile DESSERT: Margarita Jell-O Shots (lime Jell-O,
tequila, splash of triple sec)

MEXICAN BEER CHILI

This recipe can be made solo or in groups (hand each guest a margarita and a knife when he comes in the door). Accurate measurements are nowhere near necessary for this recipe. Add and subtract whatever you think best, the more chili, the spicier.

4 tablespoons olive oil
2 medium onions (one yellow and one red)
1 leek
4 garlic cloves, minced
2 or 3 teaspoons of chili powder
2 or 3 teaspoons crushed chili flakes
1 or 2 tablespoons ground cumin
1 small eggplant, peeled and diced
1 cup each black, kidney, garbanzo beans
    (properly soaked overnight, then simmered
    until tender)
(2) 20-oz. cans whole tomatoes, chopped (as
    roughly or finely as you like)

A few bottles of your favorite Mexican beer, like Negra Modelo, Dos Equis or Dos Equis Amber (English ales work well in this recipe too).
1 or 2 lbs. free-range organic chicken or organic firm-style tofu (or both), sliced
2 bell peppers (one green and one yellow), cored, seeded and cut into strips

1. Heat olive oil in a heavy-bottomed pot on low. Add onions, leek, minced garlic, chilis and cumin. Cover about 15 minutes until the onions are golden. **2.** Add eggplant, re-cover the pot and cook another 15 minutes. **3.** Add beans, tomatoes, beer. Cover and cook over medium heat for half an hour. **4.** Reduce heat to low, uncover pot slightly and let bubble until beans are soft and edible (could be two or three hours). **5.** When you think the chili is about $1/2$ hour away from begin done, add the chicken and/or tofu and bell peppers.

ALL-GUY-PARTY STANDBY: PICK UP THE PHONE AND ORDER.

Drinking Games 4

I Never

Buzz level: Low

Number of players: Unlimited

What's needed: Drinks, some brave honesty and an open mind

This version of Truth or Dare may seem a little girly, but it can definitely go down a more macho (even blowhard) road. It's perfect to get the party started and is best played among close friends . . . although it can be a great ice-breaker when played by guys who don't know each other too well.

How to play: Everyone sits in a circle. The best man goes first—and sets the tone—by saying, "I never . . ." and completes the sentence with a true statement. For example, "I never . . . um . . . had sex with that inflatable love doll at my bachelor party." This is where the game gets interesting. If someone in the crowd *has* done what the best man says he hasn't done, then that person drinks. The drinker is in no way required to give an explanation, he just drinks and the game moves on. The man to the left of the best man goes next, and so on.

How to win: There are neither winners nor losers (in the gaming sense anyway) in *I Never*, but you might think about using some inside information you have to goad some of your fellow players into drinking.

Guess the Note

Buzz level: Low

Number of players: Unlimited

What's needed: Bottled beer and a musical instrument (piano is best)

The musically inclined will truly excel at this game of ear and beer.

How to play: 1. One player sits at the instrument of choice. 2. Everyone else takes a nice swig of beer from his bottle. 2. The first player blows across the mouth of his bottle, making a note. 3. The player at the piano has three tries to match the note. If he's successful, the bottle player must take a drink. If the player at the piano is unsuccessful at matching the note, he takes three drinks and gives up his seat at the piano to the next player.

What if this mixture do not work at all?

ROMEO AND JULIET, ACT IV SCENE III

Dirty Ditties

Limericks

There was a young maid from Madras
Who had a magnificent ass
Not rounded and pink
As you probably think
It was gray, had long ears, and ate grass

A giddy young female at Yale
Was tattooed with her prices for tail
And on her behind
For the Sake of the blind
A duplicate version in Braille

A lady athletic and handsome
Got wedged in her sleeping room transom
When she offered much gold
For release she was told
The view was worth more than the ransom

A very nice fellow called Fender
Took a young girl on a bender
She said she was caught
She got but naught
'Cause Fender was opposite gender

A girl with an innocent soul
Had an idea exceedingly droll
At a masquerade ball
Dressed in nothing at all
She backed in as a Parker House roll

There was a young woman of Twickenham
Loved sausages, never got sick of 'em
Every night, every day
She'd constantly pray
To lengthen and strengthen and thicken 'em

A lesbian once in Rangoon
Asked a fairy into her room
They spent the whole night
In a hell of a fight
As to which should do what and to whom

There once was a lady from Exeter
Who made all the men crane their necks at her
And some who were brave
Would take out and wave
The distinguishing marks of their sex at her

There was a young fellow named Skinner
Took a young lady to dinner
Dined about nine
Had a wonderful time
Around about ten it was in 'er
    (not Skinner . . . the dinner)

112

Stag Gifts
CLASSIC GAGS

Presenting the bachelor with goofy gifts that will embarrass and/or delight him on his last night of freedom is a time-honored tradition. Not only are they an excellent way to get the shenanigans started, but they make great souvenirs and, if chosen wisely, some—like the Hot Sex Dice—may even delight the bride.

CUSTOMIZED M&Ms They won't print anything "vulgar or offensive," so be creative. (mymms.com)

ADULT SUPER SPERM COSTUME Comes with jumpsuit with briefs, padded headpiece and tail; one size fits . . . most adults. (FindCostume.com; 800-784-0899)

INFLATABLE WIFE Described as the perfect mate: totally silent, spends no money, leaves the toilet seat up, is totally faithful . . . and even floats. (Spencers; spencersonline.com; 800-527-7977)

Gag Gifts

PIN THE BOOBS ON THE BABE GAME Based on the classic Pin The Tail On the Donkey game of yesteryear; unlimited players. (Nawty Things; nawtythings.com; 800-779-8077)

THE PECKER EXERCISER (available in original or Glow-in-the-Dark) Beef up your most important muscle. (The Prank Store; theprankstore.com; 503-623-2854)

HOT SEX DICE One die has a body part . . . the other an action. (California Exotic Novelties; calexotics.com)

PEEPSHOW SHOT GLASSES R-rated images that are invisible until you pour a shot! Available in cheesecake (women) or beefcake (men). (Fred & Friends; fredandfriends.com)

CHICK-MAGNET COSTUME A little on the corny side, this costume nonetheless promises you'll "be the life of the party." (Prankplace. com; 800-901-1163)

CONDOM CAP Just think how zany the groom will look in this giant-sized condom hat. (Condomania; condomania.com; 800-926-6366)

GROOM'S COUNTDOWN CLOCK Counts down the days, hours, minutes and seconds to the bachelor's day of reckoning; the clock works for any date through the year 2049—for the seriously commitment challenged. (Countdown Clocks International; countdowntime.com; 888-313-2001)

DIRTY MINDS The game of naughty clues. . . . Sample: I'm a four letter word, I'm a name for a woman, I end in u-n-t, what am I? Get your mind out of the gutter and you might win. (TDC Games; tdcgames.com; 800-292-7676)

BUTTHEAD! Hours of fun are to be had with this 'grippy' hat and 3 balls that stick to it. (Perpetual Kid; perpetualkid.com; 888-282-7115)

REMOTE-CONTROLLED FART MACHINE Simply press the remote button and set off one of 15 different fart sounds from up to 100 feet away—let the embarrassment begin! (The Fart Machine; thefartmachine.com; 800-787-6227)

BEER BELT Never be thirsty again with this fully adjustable belt; holds up to 6 beers. (Baron Bob; baronbob.com; 800-788-1957)

I was the best man

at the wedding.

If I'm the best

man, why is she

marrying him?

—Jerry Seinfeld

Stag Gifts
GROOVY

Beyond the gag-gift antics that accompany the classic bachelor party, it has become more popular in recent years to bestow the groom-to-be with something a bit more substantial. From the silly to the sublime, this token should be a reflection of the bachelor's tastes, and be a step up from, let's say, a mooning lawn gnome or boobie slippers. When the gags have all played out, surprise the stag with this memento from his bachelor-year buddies.

ELECTRONIC DRINK CADDIE It looks like a regulation golf driver, but the secret is the one-button dispensing pump. Fill with hot or cold beverages, holds 54 oz. (Brookstone; brookstone.com; 866-576-7337)

DESIGN YOUR OWN SNEAKERS Make something special for the groom. (Converse; Converse.com; 888-792-3307)

FIGHTER PILOT SIMULATOR Engage in virtual mid-air combat dogfights, or for a couple grand more, do the real thing with the Air Combat Dogfight gift. (Xperience Days Inc.; xperience-days.com; 866-973-7436)

DORK SQUAD 35mm-to-digital film converter • tape deck digitizer • gag cockroaches (that "realistically creep down" any smooth, hard vertical surface. Dorks get married, too. (X-treme Geek; X-tremegeek.com; 800-480-4335)

THE GENUINE LOST IN SPACE® B-9™ ROBOT Danger Will Robinson! This *ultimate* toy will put a real dent in your wallet. The groom's beloved might not appreciate the fact that it's faithfully reproduced from original archival blueprints, but he will. (Hammacher Schlemmer; hammacher.com; 800-321-1484)

CIGAR-TASTING EXPERIENCE Learn how to choose, cut, light, smoke and store your stogies; one-on-one expert instruction. (Excitations; excitations.com; 877-839-2483)

WINE, BEER, COFFEE, CHEESE, STEAK, OLIVE OIL, HOT SAUCE, NECKTIE OR EVEN DOG TREAT OF THE MONTH CLUB. (AmazingClubs. com; 800-507-4660)

GAME-ON Monogrammed Poker Chips • MLB Billiard Balls • NFL Billiard Balls • Arcade Games: From cards to Ms. Pac-Man, these gifts are for the gaming boy. (Frontgate; frontgate.com; 888-263-9850)

Drinking Games 5

Bachelor-Boy Jeopardy

Buzz level: Moderate

Number of players: One M.C., unlimited contestants (split into teams)

What's needed: The best man to act as host and M.C., personalized trivia questions, pen and paper to write down your answers

How to play: 1. The best man prepares a series of trivia questions about the bachelor boy separated into categories such as work, play, pets, fashion, girlfriends past and present—whatever makes sense. 2. The contestants are split into teams and draw straws to see which goes first. 3. The team that goes first chooses a category and the M.C. reads a question. 4. Each team writes down an answer and reveals it when the M.C. calls on them. 5. Teams with an incorrect answer have to drink. If every team gets the answer right, the groom has to drink. 6. The M.C. then asks one of the teams that got the answer right to choose the next category. If no one got it right, the groom picks the next category.

Scoring: 100 points for each correct answer; 1000 points wins.

VARIATION 1: If you have live entertainment (e.g. a stripper or boxing dwarfs) the best man can create on-the-spot bonus questions, like "What was the last dancer's name?" or "What was the stripper wearing . . . in terms of jewelry?"

VARIATION 2: Create combo bachelor and entertainment bonus questions like, "What aspect of Bambi's performance did the bachelor boy find most fascinating? Be specific please." (Don't forget to check with the groom to get the answers first).

But, soft! Methinks I scent the morning air.

HAMLET, ACT I SCENE V

ACTIVITY

CUSTOMIZED T-SHIRTS!

Use these unique designs to make a set of T-shirts the whole stag party can wear. Customize as needed, then enlarge and transfer the image using dry-transfer paper and a copier. Iron on following the package directions.

6'0"

5'6"

5'0"

4'6"

Place headshot of the stag here.

LAST NIGHT OF FREEDOM

STAG NAME

MARRIED: 06/21/2009

SENTENCE: LIFE

Customize the panel with details about the soon-to-be-incarcerated stag—and don't forget to add his face!

STAG NIGHT

See you in hell!

VEGAS STAG

LET 'EM RIDE

STAG NIGHT
THE BUCK STOPS HERE!

Place headshot of the stag here.

JOHN'S LAST NIGHT OF FREEDOM 06/21/2009

Customize with the stag's name and wedding date.

SMOKIN' PARTY SCHEMES

There's nothing inherently wrong with painting a dwarf blue and chaining him to your best friend, drinking till you drop, ogling someone's . . . whatever . . . or getting a lap dance—they're tried-and-true crowd pleasers. But using a little ingenuity and thinking outside the box (so to speak) can be more fulfilling—especially for the bachelor. Mix and match these alternatives to suit your stag's tastes and be the envy of all those bachelors who've gone before. And, if you're clever enough, a stripper or dwarf can be incorporated into practically any festivity.

Sail the Caribbean 🔆 Build a Room, a Shed, a House 🔆 A Day at the Horse Races 🔆 Camp in the Green Mountains, the White Mountains, the desert, Iceland 🔆 Hike the Appalachian Trail 👍 Go deep sea fishing 🔆 Mountain climbing 🔆 Do a day at the ball park 🔆 Learn karate 🔆 Plant a garden 🔆 Learn to surf 👍 Attend a Las Vegas boxing match 👍 Bike across the state 🔆 Do a day at the spa 🔆 Soak in a mud, Russian or Turkish bath 🔆 Canyoneer 🔆 Spelunk 👍 Swim with sharks 👍 Learn SCUBA 🔆 Take a private tour of the Metropolitan Museum of Art 👍 Bungee jump 🔆 Raft the rapids 🔆 Raft the Grand Canyon 👍 Mountain Bike 🔆 Zip-line the jungle 👍 Be a ghetto tourist 👍 Have a day of video games 🔆 Volunteer at a soup kitchen, an archeological site, the botanical gardens, as a hawk watch volunteer at Acadia National Park or on a Red Cross humanitarian mission 👍 Host a bowling tournament 🔆 Do an entire weekend of Dungeons & Dragons 🔆 Stage a BBQ cook-off 👍 Design and build a tree house -☀- Zorb® 👍 Have a movie marathon: film noir, sci-fi, disaster, Tarentino, Hitchcock, Altman, or 70s porn -☀- Take a wine tasting course -☀- Do Disneyland, paintball, the roller-coasters of the East -☀- Foxhunt -☀- Cliff dive in Mexico: observe or participate 👍 Attend the Indy 500, the Kentucky Derby, the Super Bowl, the French Open, the World Cup, the Olympics, the Iditarod -☀- Cross-country ski Yellowstone -☀- Attend the World Championship Hog-Calling Contest 👍 The running of the bulls: observe or participate -☀- Dogsled -☀- Bullfights: observe or participate -☀- Do Six Flags 👍 Ululate at the Camel Wrestling Festival in Selçuk, Turkey -☀- Compete in a marathon -☀- Enjoy a weekend of Broadway -☀- Take an improv class 👍 Do a spirituality weekend 👍 Learn tantra yoga -☀- Take in a night of stand-up -☀- Go out cigar tasting -☀- Take a cooking class, a mixology course, a beer appreciation course -☀- Golf Pebble Beach -☀- Join a life drawing class -☀- Take a circus arts class (juggling, trapeze, tumbling) 👍 Learn the elements of jazz -☀- Learn to ride a motorcycle -☀- Have a dinner party (from cocktails to smokes & brandy) followed by poker 👍 Stage a poker tournament -☀- Learn to ballroom dance 👍 Attend a film festival, a jazz festival -☀- Take a wine tour of Napa, Argentina, Chile, Germany, Greece or South Africa -☀- Set up a one-on-one basketball tournament, a billiards tournament -☀- Go game hunting

129

ZORB®-ING*

The practice of humans traveling in a sphere, generally made of transparent plastic, usually for fun.

What guy hasn't dreamed of having a giant ball to run around in like his childhood pet hamster? And who knew such an activity had a name—zorbing*—and that it is actually a popular event for bachelor get-togethers?

Started in New Zealand in the mid-90s by two guys who were looking for a way to walk on water, zorbing* comes in three basic forms: with water on the inside so you can slide along as the ball rolls down a hill; with a harness so you tumble with the ball as it goes downhill; and on water (a lake, pond or, for the very brave, rapids) so the rider has to walk to get the ball rolling.

So far this sport is practiced mostly in countries where worrying about safety ranks a distant second to having a good time. The first location in the United States opened in 2007 in Pigeon Forge, Tennessee (also the home of Dollywood), but look for more outlets to follow.

To see a video, check out www.zorb.com/smoky or call (865) 428-2422 for details.

According to the Guinness Book of World Records in 2006:

Longest ride is held by Steve Camp, who traveled 570 meters (1,900 ft).

Fastest ride is held by Keith Kolver, who reached a speed of 52 kilometers per hour (32 mph).

*Zorbing is also known as sphereing or sometimes globeriding. The Zorb® Globe is the proper name of the ride-in ball.

Slightly Naughty
JOKES!

A salesman was looking for his buddy, George Sexhour. He went to the hotel, walked up to the girl at the desk, and asked, "Do you have Sexhour here?"

"Mister," she replied, "we don't even get a coffee break!"

He held her close against him, a burning glow of satisfaction going through them.

"Am I the first man you ever made love to?" he panted.

"You must be," she said, studying him closely. "Your face looks very familiar."

The circus manager's wife was considerably upset when she entered their trailer unexpectedly and found her husband sleeping with the lady midget.

"You promised me a month ago that you would never cheat on me again," she cried.

Her husband simply shrugged and said, "Well as you can see, I'm tapering off."

Mary had an aeroplane,
In it, she loved to frisk.
Now, wasn't she a silly girl,
Her little *.

A young widow sued a young man in a paternity case. In the trial, the judge asked, "Did you ever sleep with this woman?"

"Not a wink, Your Honor," said the man. "Not a wink."

It was late at night when the doorbell rang. The madam of the house answered it and saw a man standing with his arms and legs in plaster casts.

"I want a woman," he said.

"Look," said the madam, "go on home. It's late and I want to get some sleep."

"But I want a woman," he repeated.

"Let's be realistic. What could you do with a woman in your condition?"

"Listen, lady, I rang the bell, didn't I?"

Home after a long absence overseas with the Armed Forces, Hannegan was most suspicious of his beloved wife's conduct during his long time away from home. She protested her innocence for a long time, but finally she broke down and admitted committing an infidelity while Hannegan was abroad.

"Who was it?" the outraged husband demanded. "Was it that heel O'Brien?"

His wife shook her head.

"Was it Brady?" he thundered.

"No, no! Not Brady!" she replied.

"Was it O'Hara? . . . Was it Finnegan? . . . Was it Burns? . . . Was it Murphy?" Hannegan frothed on. But his wife continued to shake her head stubbornly.

"So!" Hannegan exploded at last. "None of my friends is good enough for you!"

A nervous young man couldn't keep his eyes off the ample bust of the girl selling him tickets at a railroad station.

"Will you stop staring at my bust and tell me where you want a ticket to?" the annoyed girl asked.

Gulping, the man replied, "Just give me two pickets to Tittsburgh."

Thanks to a fortuitous breakdown of his car, Jimmy found himself alone for the night in a motel room with Suzi, his current heart's desire. However, despite the golden opportunity for romance, Suzi, who had produced and donned a black nightgown, proved unexpectedly obdurate to his advances, stubbornly resisting his every effort to lift the enticing, semi-transparent, flimsy garment above her dimpled knees.

Finally, in a state of high frustration, Jimmy flung himself from the room, cursing Suzi and all her sex. Suzi promptly locked the door, and none too soon, for moments later, Jimmy was back, rattling the knob and knocking furiously.

"If you don't open up," he cried, "I'm going to break down this door."

"Huh!" cried Suzi in derision. "First you can't lift a flimsy nightgown, now you're going to break down a door!"

"ELBOWS ON THE TABLE AGAIN! WHERE ARE YOUR MANNERS?

STRANGE (YES)... BUT *TRUE*?

Because what happens at a bachelor party tends to stay at a bachelor party, stories—especially true ones—are few and far between. Everyone says they have great bachelor party stories to tell but they never seem to come forth with them. Maybe it's the stag party code of silence, or maybe the wild and debauched party is just a macho myth and parties tend to be more like the average baby shower. Here are some stories (along with the handcuffed blue-painted dwarf on page 99) that are circulating. You decide . . . reality or urban myth?

ALL-STAR CAST

I heard this story from a guy I worked with years ago:

He had a buddy who was a paramedic in the military and lived in a small apartment on the second story of an old house just off the base. The apartment had an outside entrance at the head of a long set of outside wooden stairs on the side of the house. He always complained about the stairs as being a pain in the butt because they did not conform to the building code. There were 32 stairs in a single flight from top to bottom. Being fairly old and wood, they were worn and extremely slippery in the winter or when it was raining.

He was afraid that one day he'd slip on them and break his neck, but the rent was cheap and he kept putting off looking for something better, knowing that he'd be posted somewhere else right after he got married.

Anyway, on the night of his stag his buddies got him roaring drunk and were considering stripping him down to his shorts and chaining him to a parking meter, but they thought that had been done and that trick was getting old.

They kept pouring him drinks until he passed out, and then they took him home and carried him upstairs, unconscious. Being a paramedic, he had his crash kit at home that was full of all sorts of medical supplies, so while he was out they put him in a full-length leg cast and left him there.

In the morning they went back and told him the he had fallen down the stairs and broken his leg. He said he couldn't remember a thing after about the third bar that he was in, but that for a broken leg, it felt pretty good. They had to cut the leg of his dress uniform so he could get his pants on. He got married in that cast, much to the chagrin of his bride and her mother, but he got a lot of sympathy from everybody else. All of their pictures were taken with him sitting down or on crutches and they only told him it was a joke as they were driving off on the honeymoon. She didn't talk to to the perpetrators of the stunt for two years. In fact, she wouldn't even let them in the house for about six months.

—*From R.C., Swan Lake, NY*

SAILOR SVEN

In Sweden it is a bit of a custom for the groom to be kidnapped and whisked off somewhere for his stag night, which usually lasts all day and all night rather than the typical British stag night, where you all arrange it beforehand, go out, get drunk and hire a stripper.

The Swedes do it different. The groom has no idea until he gets nabbed. He might be dressed up in something crazy . . . and go do something funny . . . and then the fun starts!

This particular guy is a keen sailor and when he was kidnapped for his stag night they pasted a false skipper's beard on him, put him at the helm of a 60-foot yacht and let him be skipper for the day. . . . Much beer and fine food was consumed. But nothing nasty happened to him at all. . . .

In the evening when they got back on land and were getting cleaned up for the nightclub . . . they all had a sauna as is customary in Sweden. . . .

Imagine the groom's horror when he walked into the sauna where his naked buddies were waiting for him and notice that best mate number one had no pubic hair.

Neither did friend two . . . nor three . . . nor four. . . .

Now check out the false beard again. . . .

—From the Web site SoVeryWrong.com

RINKY DINK PANTHER

In a land far away in a time not so long ago there was a stag weekend in full swing. All the chaps were dressed in suitably ridiculous attire; I myself was dressed in a pink panther suit.

To set the record straight, I wasn't the stag—just a crazy fool who has no self-control when it comes to drinking, showing off and being the center of attention. I was at the time a single chap and ready to sow my seed as much as possible over the coming three days of fun. The night had begun in full swing—well, it had really begun as an afternoon session and just blurred into the nighttime session.

We were in the third drinking establishment of the evening and I was well and truly lubed. The silver tongued patter was rolling of the tongue, at this point to no avail. Out the corner of my eye I spotted two honeys, real stunners; in the name of all things good and right these girls needed some of my charm and attention, and if they were lucky, some of my lovin' later.

I grabbed the first available wing man, this happened to be Barney Rubble, and off we went. Drinks were offered and accepted, small talk and witty anecdotes were exchanged, all stations were go and ready for take off. Things were going fantastic, until it started: the spinning, stomach spasms, and dizziness, the feeling of all things evil rising from the pit of your stomach further and further. I was out of the door quicker than a scouser [someone from Liverpool] out of the door on giro day [unemployment check day].

I just couldn't hold it in anymore. I ran for the bushes and began throwing up like crazy. My head in the bushes and my arse pointing at all the people, pink tail wagging and all. I just couldn't stop throwing up, when suddenly severe cramps in my lower regions took hold of me, then to my horror I started shitting all over myself. It was a disaster. Drunk as I was, I didn't know whether to turn and vomit to their faces or keep shitting there until it came out down my furry pink pants. The saddest part of this story is that later I was told that this really beautiful, foxy, large-chested sort was going to bang me like a shit-house door in a gale.

Instead of an all-night session of toe curling and scream-ing, I had the indignity of the long walk home in my now not so pink and fluffy suit, shit and puke stains for all to see. Needless to say I took a huge amount of piss for the next few years, and as hard as I tried I didn't get my deposit back from the fancy dress shop.

—From the Web site SoVeryWrong.com

Mexican Trip

Be especially wary of holding bachelor parties in foreign countries even if it is just Mexico.

The girls may be cheaper but the local police may not understand "bachelor party" and "I was only kidding around" while they are smacking you over the head with empty Tequila bottles. If Mexico fits into the party plans, assign at least two people, preferably ones who speak Spanish, to ensure you get back across the border in time for the wedding.

—from *Great Bachelor Parties* by Herb Kavet

"SOMETIMES I GET THE IMPRESSION THEY'RE UNDRESSING US IN THEIR MINDS."

Man-Hungry Amazons of Tabasco

by Crain Matheson

I think the Lacandon Indian tried to murder me, but maybe he was only trying to save his own life. We were halfway across the jungle pool when he suddenly tipped the narrow dugout canoe and tumbled me into the water at the same time that I heard a strange babble of noises behind us. They sounded like women's voices, but I didn't have time to look back because I was trying not to drown. My heavy pack and weapons dragged me down, and I gulped a bellyful of swamp water. I had to rip off most of my equipment under water, and when at last I surfaced, I couldn't swim because my arms and legs kept getting tangled in the water hyacinths. I yelled like hell in Spanish. The Lacandon glanced over his shoulder, and I saw terror in his eyes. He paddled furiously for shore. The strange babbling was still going on, and I struggled about in the water to see what had terrified him—alligators, snakes, Chamula Indians, or any one of a dozen other jungle horrors . . .

It was women. Several canoeloads of gals. And they were paddling for all they were worth, heading straight for me!

But so were a couple of dozen deadly pit vipers of the water moccasin type, slithering across the hyacinths like huge yellow worms with black stripes and golden eyes and white fangs. Their sting will paralyze a man within 30 seconds and kill him in a minute. They moved toward me as I yelled and beat the water, trying to frighten the snakes away, but they squirmed nearer to me from flower to flower. Fear flooded my body with power, and I thrashed through the clinging hyacinths, ripping them to shreds as I clawed my way across the water, sobbing and shouting in terror.

Then the women's boats were all around me, and long bare arms reached down to help me aboard. I clambered into the first dugout and fell exhausted in the bottom.

The women swarmed over me then, stripping off my clothes and turning me this way and

143

Man-Hungry Amazons of Tabasco

that, inspected my body for snakebites. Finding none, they continued examining me, feeling me all over and chattering in their Indian dialect. The girls giggled and tittered as they ran their hands over my body.

And in the back of my mind I began to get an idea. Where were the men? These were not Lacandon women, nor Chamulas. They looked something like the Tehuanas of Tehuantepec and Juchitan, very pretty and gay, and half naked, bare to the waist and wearing only wraparound skirts. They were a little taller than ordinary Indian women, and they seemed strong enough to do men's work. If what I was thinking was true, I had an amazing anthropological discovery. As I did not speak their Indian dialect, I tried talking to them in Spanish.

"Donde estan sus hombres?"

"Where are your men?" I asked.

You could see by the blank expressions in their eyes that they spoke little or no Spanish. Not all citizens of the Republic of Mexico speak the language of Cortez: many thousand use only their own native Indian dialects, with perhaps a sprinkling of common Spanish words. The only word they understood was *hombres*, and they repeated it over and over, giggling and laughing and saying *hombres-hombres-hombres* in their sing-song Indian voices. Meanwhile they paddled towards shore. They stood barefoot on the gunwales of the dugouts, stroking the water with flat paddles that sent us scooting over the hyacinth-covered surface.

We beached, and while some of the women dragged the canoes into the underbrush, others clustered around me and crowded

me along with them into the jungle. It was only a short walk to their village, and I wondered how the Lacandon and I could have missed it when we passed that way earlier. I began to suspect he missed it purposely.

It was a small village of 30 palm-thatched huts. There were a few children, mostly girls, perhaps a dozen scrawny men, and about 100 women. Everyone but the few men flocked around us as we entered the village, and the women especially crowded close to me, running their hands over my body and smiling enticingly.

In the center of the village we stopped before a hut that was larger than the rest. A woman stepped out from the dark interior. She was taller than the others, fairer in complexion, her hair less straight, tending to curl where it hung far below her naked shoulders. She wore only a wraparound skirt from her waist down. Her breasts were large and firm and she was a handsome figure of a woman. She was young, about 25.

Neither of us spoke at first. We simply looked each other over. She surveyed me as frankly as one would examine a horse before buying it. We were a strange contrast in types, for she was dark and small, though taller than the other women, while I am red-haired, blue-eyed and five feet nine. I could have picked her up and held her in the palm of one hand.

The women and children were quiet now, watching us, and over their heads I could see the small group of men in a whispering knot at the edge of the crowd. They looked at me as if I was a tax collector, a kind of man proverbially hated and fre-

quently murdered in Mexico's backwaters. And if my developing theory proved correct, these scrawny, sickly men were likely to become troublesome. I wondered just how strong the women of this strange village really were. They seemed to run things, and their leader was a woman.

The woman spoke in Spanish: "Who are you?" Her voice had the musical singsong of the Indian, for she was not pure Spanish.

"My name is Crain Matheson," I answered. She looked me squarely in the eyes as we talked, the way a man might do if he were honest. I told her, I come from Chicago. . . ."

But that's as far as I got, because just then that group of scrawny males came up and tried to start trouble. I didn't understand a word they said, since

they spoke their Indian dialect, but apparently the men had some objection to make about me, for their leader kept looking at me and jabbering angrily at the lady chief. The leader of the men was a thin scar-faced man with a thin scraggy beard and broken teeth. The lady chief gave him a dis-

gusted look. She listened impatiently, then placed her hands on her hips and glared at him. For the first time I noticed that in her left hand she carried a kind of short whip.

She answered him in dialect, but I heard one word used over and over, and I gathered it was the man's name: Xochil—which is also an Aztec word meaning "Pretty One," which he wasn't.

Suddenly she lashed out, striking the man across his face. He cowered as she struck again, drawing blood this time. I knew now how his face got so scarred, no doubt from whippings. He dropped to his knees, and she lashed him again and again until he slunk away on all fours, his face bleeding form a long slash. The other men followed him.

The women laughed gleefully, but the men gathered again in an angry, chattering knot at the

edge of the village, glancing my way now and then with murderous looks. As an anthropologist I could see what had happened to make these people the way they were: Something had caused their genetic strain to produce few males and many more females, and instead of the scarcity of males giving them heightened value their weakness in numbers had merely made them more vulnerable to feminine domination. This imbalance in nature has occurred elsewhere, but usually with the result that all males are highly prized by the outnumbering and sex-starved females. For instance, the Polynesian island of Rapa, where the women outnumber the men six to one and the men are pampered by the gals. I was beginning to suspect that in this village the reversed roles of men and women had also reversed certain aspects of their sexuality. But at the moment I was thinking less as an anthropologist than as a mere man in trouble.

The lady chief snapped commands to her women, and they scattered at once, going about their duties. Then she spoke to me in Spanish, "Follow me!" She led the way into her hut.

I followed. My eyes quickly became accustomed to the darkness of the hut's interior, and I sat where she pointed, on a low pile of woven grass mats, while she threw a shapely leg over the webbing of a hammock and then lay back in it, one bare leg hanging down, her arms behind her head. She looked long and silently at me, and then she spoke again.

"Crain Matheson," she said, "from Chicago. . . . Where is this place?"

"Chicago is a city in the United States," I said, wondering just how isolated this Indian village was.

When she asked, "And what is the United States?" I knew that I was in a world lost in time. It was late October 1957, but only for me.

"The United States is a country far to the north of Mexico," I said.

"Mexico?" she echoed.

"This is Mexico," I added.

"No," she said, "this is Xiximul." Then she sat up in the hammock, and pointing towards the south she said, "There lies the land of the Lacadons. The other way lies the land of the Chamulas. All around us is the country of the chicleros. I have heard of Mexico, but it is far beyond the chicleros, far beyond the Chamulas."

"Look," I said, "Xiximul is only your village and the land about it, and all this is only a part of the state of Tabasco, and this state is only one part of Mexico."

She laughed and lay back again in the hammock, placing her arms behind her head looking frankly at me with aroused desire.

"You are a little mad," she said, "but if you will come here to me, I will make you sane again. Come!"

I obeyed. The hammock was a wide one, what in the Latin-American tropics is called the *hamaca matrimonial*, and it easily held both of us, though I was a little awkward getting into it and had to be helped. But after a moment I got the hang of the thing and found it quite comfortable.

She held me with everything that can hold a man, and her mouth devoured mine. If I had been a mouse and she a hungry cat, I would not have survived 10 seconds, but her hunger though ravenous was not fatal, and I lasted several hours. It was nightfall when at last her frantic hands grew still and her clinging arms relaxed their hold.

Then she found time for talk, and she asked questions about me and my origins, why I had come to Xiximul. . . .

"We saw you and the Lacandon," their lady chief told me, "when you passed our village, and we followed you, hoping to kill the Lacandon and capture you. When we saw him take you in the *piragua*, I knew we had you, for many women with oars can paddle faster than one little Lacandon . . . I'm sorry we did not catch him, he would have made a good meal for us. That was why he paddled so hard to get away. . . ."

I wanted to change the subject, for I could smell mouth-watering odors of cooking from somewhere, and I was getting hungry. She asked more questions about what I did, and I explained how an anthropologist studies primitives . . .

"You call me primitive!" she yelled. "I am queen of all Xiximul!"

She flipped out of the hammock then and quickly took her short whip from its hanging place on one of the hammock poles, whirled around at me and began striking out.

I caught the whip across my bare chest and grabbed her, pinning her arms with mine and falling with her onto the pile of grass mats. I held her down with my body while she raged in Spanish and Indian and struggled like a tigress. She was amazingly strong for a small woman, and I

really had my hands full. But at last she grew quiet. She lay still, and looked into my eyes with a look other than anger.

I got up then and stood over her. But she stayed on the mats, still looking up at me.

She whispered, *"Mi amor."*

I reached down and pulled her up to me, and she put her arms around my neck and lay her head against my chest quietly. This was the queen of Xiximul!

After the feast, Queen Tesia made a speech to the women. I tried to gather the gist of what she was saying to them by watching their faces, but all I could guess was that she was talking about me, for they gave me sidelong looks that could only have meant one thing.

Then the speech was over. Tesia took me by the hand, and we returned to her hut. She was a very desirable young woman, and I was not unwilling to crawl into the hammock with her again, but this wasn't what she had in mind.

Tesia had told me about the system they had devised for using the males. With consiaderable fear I saw that system was about to come into play. Six of the younger women entered the hut behind us, and when I was about to climb into Tesia's hammock with her, they crowded around me, whipping off their wraparound skirts and pressing close.

Tesia said "These girls want you, too. You must help them."

"All six of them?" I said. I could see how the males of Xiximul became so weak and sickly. Sheer overwork.

"All six," Tesia replied. "And six more tomorrow. It is our system when we find a strong

male. It is a long time since we have had a male who can handle more than one woman a day, or even one. But you are fresh and strong, and I know that you do not tire quickly. You will breed tall, red-haired sons like yourself. If you do not fail, you can become chief of Xiximul. . . ."

Meanwhile the six girls were wasting no time. Pressing close to me, they pushed me backwards onto the pile of grass mats, and in a rotation best understood by them, they began the work of breeding, as if I were merely a

stud horse and they were broodmares.

I won't pretend that I resisted, even though I knew what the end of all this had to be—utter exhaustion for me, and therefore weakness before my enemies, the other men—for the girls were as desirable as young Indian women usually are, and after all I am a man. At last the six girls finished their work, and I lay upon the mats as weak as a kitten. I wondered if I could stand the pace if this same thing was to happen every day, as Tesia said. 🍥

Las Vegas

Stag Travel

The ultimate party town where anything can happen and anything that does happen will not (keep your fingers crossed) follow you home. There's plenty to drink, there are plenty of girls in various states of undress, there are boxing matches, star chefs, luxurious spas, bad lounge singers, outdoor sports and the beautiful roulette wheel. It is a ready-made bachelor-party paradise.

Use the categories below as a rough guide, then mix and match—geeky he-man, maybe, or hipster second (or more) marriage—depending on where you fall in the spectrum.

He-Man

Stay: PALMS (866-942-7777; palms.com)—the Bunnies at the Playboy Club located on the 52nd floor are only an elevator ride away; or CAESARS PALACE (866-227-5938; www.harrahs.com)—with blockbuster entertainment downstairs and a six-room "party pad," media center and dance floor upstairs, you are king here. **Eat:** DELMONICO STEAK HOUSE (Venetian Hotel; 702-414-3737)—Emeril Lagasse serves up rib-eyes and fine wines at his down-and-dirty steakhouse; BUFFET BELLAGIO (Bellagio Hotel; 702-693-8255)—from Buffalo wings to wild boar and everything in between; MEMPHIS CHAMPIONSHIP BARBECUE (1401 South Rainbow Blvd.; 702-254-0520 and 2250 East Warm Springs Road; 702-260-6909)—ribs, pulled-pork and all the fixin's at this award-winning BBQ. **Play:** X BURLESQUE (Flamingo Hotel; 800-221-7299)—X-girls, bungees and bathtubs combine to create cheesy and sleezy fun; BODY ENGLISH (Hard Rock Hotel; 702-693-4000)—the testosterone flows at this hyper-masculine nightclub; MOON (702-942-6832)—a boutique nightclub with a retractable roof; the PLAYBOY CLUB (702-944-3464)—where Bunnies serve drinks as you gamble; and RAIN (702-942-6832)—with headliners, a dance floor and "intimate enclaves," water, fog and fireballs, skyboxes, haze and "water booths" . . . wow! All three at the Palms. **Daytime:** The RICHARD PETTY DRIVING EXPERIENCE at the Las Vegas Motor Speedway (800-644-4444; lvms.com)—race like the pros in a V-8 NASCAR style racecar.

Urban Hipster

Dwell: WYNN (877-321-WYNN or 702-770-7000; wynnhotel.com)—rooms like stylish apartments found in Manhattan or London, and swimming pools like a Bel Air mansion; the FOUR SEASONS (800-819-5053; fourseasons.com/lasvegas)—an oasis of calm—no ringing slot machines—and a spa with a Zen lounge. **Top Tables:** L'ATELIER DE JOËL ROBUCHON (MGM Hotel; 702-891-7358)—casual-but-spectacular New French cuisine; CRAVINGS (Mirage Hotel; 702-791-7111)—the ultimate buffet in a groovy cafeteria setting; IN-N-OUT BURGER (various locations around town)—eat in or take out the best fast food in the West. **Amusements:** ZUMANITY (New York-New York Hotel; 866-606-7111)—Cirque du Soleil's sexy show; MGM Grand's CRAZY HORSE PARIS (MGM Grand Hotel; 877-880-0880)—sensuous choreography + light displays + film + women = "sexy perfected"; BEAUTY BAR (517 Fremont Street; 702-598-1965; beautybar.com)—escape from the gargantuan casinos on the Strip to this eclectic bar in historic downtown; DOUBLE DOWN SALOON (4640 Paradise Road; 702-791-5775; doubledownsaloon.com)—a dive-bar antidote to the glitz of Las Vegas and birthplace of the bacon martini.

Daytime: Tour and taste test at the DON PABLO CIGAR COMPANY (3049 Las Vegas South, #25; 702-369-1818) or ETHEL M CHOCOLATES (2 Cactus Garden Drive, Henderson, NV; 702-435-2655; ethelschocolate.com); mountain bike, rock climb or see wildflowers at nearby RED ROCK CANYON (redrockcanyonlv.org; 702-515-5350).

Geek

Habitat: STRATOSPHERE (800-998-6937; stratospherehotel.com)—ride the giant teeter-totter as it goes over the edge of the 110-story tower or live your knight-in-shining-armor fantasies at EXCALIBUR (877-750-5464; excalibur.com). **Nourishment:** TAO (Venetian Hotel; 702-388-8338)—besides the awesome pan-Asian cuisine, there's WiFi; TOURNAMENT OF KINGS "JOUSTING" DINNER SHOW (Excalibur Hotel; 702-597-7600)—invading armies, dancing maidens and eating with your fingers; CHIPOTLE (various locations)—this Mexican chain offers "spaceship-size burritos." **Merrymaking:** EYE-CANDY SOUND LOUNGE & BAR (Mandalay Bay Hotel; 702-632-7777)—with high-tech fiber optics and interactive multi-touch tables, you create images and project them over the dance floor, change the music and send messages to other dorks—all from the comfort of your booth; HOOKAH LOUNGE (8380 W. Sahara Avenue; 702-731-6030)—smoke hookah pipes and pretend you're on Tatooine. **Daytime:** STAR TREK: THE EXPERIENCE (Hilton Hotel; 888-GO-BOLDLY; startrekexp.com)—go forth and prosper . . . or at least spend the day living in the 24th century; KING TUT'S TOMB (Luxor Hotel; 702-262-4444)—explore the world of the boy king.

2nd (or more) Marriage

Room: It's your second (or more) time around—try a new and exciting country (or at least a hotel with a foreign theme): MONTE CARLO (888-529-4828; montecarlo.com); PARIS (877-603-4386; parislasvegas.com) or THE VENETIAN (877-883-6423; venetian.com). **Board:** These are more Rat-Pack and less glitter: ANDRÉ'S (401 S. Sixth Street; 702-385-5016; andrelv.com)—classic French cuisine served up in a charming converted house; HUGO'S CELLAR (Four Queens Hotel, 202 Fremont Street; 702-385-4011; hugos cellar.com)—relive the 70s with steaks, seafood and flaming cherries jubilee prepared tableside; CAPITAL GRILLE (Fashion Show Mall, 3200 Las Vegas Blvd. S.; 702-932-6631; thecapital grille.com)—the no-frills dark-wood-and-brass

décor is far from the typical Las Vegas glamour, but still, they are "the masters of steak." **Recreation:** DOWNTOWN COCKTAIL ROOM (111 Las Vegas Blvd. South; 702-880-DOWN; down townlv.net)—no themes, no scenes, just a casual crowd and cool music; SPEARMINT RHINO (3340 South Highland Drive, 702-796-3600; spearmintrhinolv.com)—often voted best gentleman's club by the local community, they have lapdance-friendly chairs, too. Take in some Classic Headliners like Don Rickles, Bette Midler, Tom Jones, Roseanne Barr, Chris Rock, Bill Cosby, Jay Leno, Jerry Seinfeld, even Donny & Marie (. . . but only if the groom absolutely insists). **Daytime:** WILD WEST SUNSET DINNER BBQ (877-WILDWST; wildwesthorsebackadventures. com)—saddle up and be a cowpoke for the day; finish with a fireside BBQ dinner or spend the day rafting on the COLORADO RIVER (ask your concierge to hook you up).

Mating Call

BERTRAM GARILL ALIAS "BENNIE THE GONIFF" SPENDS MOST OF HIS TIME BETWEEN ALCATRAZ AND LAS VEGAS CULTIVATING VEGETABLES ... HIS LATEST, A TOMATO NAMED BUSTY BELLE ... FORMERLY A NEW ORLEANS SWAMP FIRE, NOW BURNING THEM UP IN A HOLLYWOOD BURLYQUE SPOT

I CAN'T APPRECIATE SUCH ELEGANT TOIPSECHORE WITH ALL THESE BUMS MAKING WITH VULGAR NOISES!

WOW! TAKE IT OFF!

LET IT GO!

WHER

BOSS, YOU WANT WHAT WE SHOULD SHUTTEMUP!

LEAVE US NOT INCITE THE HOOLIGANS ... OR THE COPS ... CONVINCE MISS BUSTY BELLE SHE SHOULD GIVE A PRIVATE PERFORMANCE AT THE TALUGA TOWERS APARTMENT 3A

COME ON PIGEON, YOU'RE BOOKED FOR A SOLO "CHEZ BENNIE"!

GENTLEMEN! GET YO COTTON PICKIN HAND OFF MAH NATURAL EQUIP ...

MAX, GET THIS HEARSE TO MAKE LIKE A HOT-ROD!

INTRODUCIN' FOR YOUR PERSONAL PLEASURE, OUR NEXT FEATURE DIRECT FROM THE SOUTH ... BUSTY BELLE!

JUST WATCH YOUR HANDS BACK THERE MISTER!

MAYBE SOME HOT JAZZ ON THE RADIO WILL HELP PUT OUR DOLL IN A DANCING MOOD

Y'ALL WASTING TIME, AH JUST NEVER DO BENEFITS OR ONE MAN SHOWS!

AND THIS ROD SAYS YOU DO! -- NO WORDS NO MUSIC-JUST BUMPS AND GRINDS!

THIS IS AS FAR AS AH STRIP UNLESS AH'M IN LOVE!

SKIP THE ADVICE TO THE LOVELORN -- I WANT THEM PANTIES OFF TOO!

SINCE YOU WANT THEM SO BADLY ... HERE THEY ARE!

HEY!

NOW AH'VE GOT THE SHOOTIN IRON ... AND YOU'LL DANCE FOR MAH PLEASURE!

Stag Travel
Leaving Las Vegas

Though stag parties occur every day all 'round the world in large towns and small, at local bars and in church basements (yes, it happens), it's always nice to take your posse on the road for one last hurrah before tying the knot. And while Las Vegas (see page 152) is perpetually among the top destinations, here are a few other—more esoteric—ideas.

Berlin Come to the cabaret—the nightlife in Berlin is legendary (no pesky rules about drinking hours). Take a Trabi Safari (trabi-safari.de) in the classic Eastern European car of yesteryear to get your bearings in the city.

Bratislava Good beer, inexpensive (especially for those with sterling or euros), and quaint. This is a fast growing stag destination for Europeans (especially the lads from Britain). Party over water at Cirkus Barok (cirkusbarok.sk) or underground in a former nuclear fallout shelter at Subclub (subclub.sk).

Cabo San Lucas Take a left at Los Angeles and keep going till you come to the end of North America. Here you'll find dramatic beauty, sandy beaches, azure water and some really big fish waiting to be caught. Oh yeah, and a *loco* nightlife, too.

Cancún Cheap vacation packages draw spring breakers and bachelor blowouts alike. But beyond the strippers and endless Coronas (and whatever else you get up to), there's the Caribbean on one side and the Nichupte Lagoon (ideal for water sports) on the other.

Ibiza This long-time Spanish party destination's nightlife—think soul, funk, trance—is the draw. Daytime recovery is found swimming or playing in the Mediterranean, then it's tapas and dancing under the stars (amnesia-ibiza.com).

Krakow Long trumpeted by stag partiers as "the new Prague," this Polish city is known for its

A MEXICAN "BELLE
TIJUANA MEXICO

beer and vodka. It also claims to have the highest density of bars in the world (no designated driver needed) mixed with a very young population. Go-carting and shooting Kalashnikovs (yes, AK-47s) are among the more unique activities on tap.

Ljubljana

Too many consonants in a row, you might be thinking, but others love the cheap booze, skiing, Baroque architecture and hovercrafting (be George Jetson) available in and around this picturesque and cosmopolitan European city.

Montréal

Because Canadian law allows touching (between dancer and customer and between dancers *themselves—oh, la, la!*) as long as it does not "constitute a sexual exchange like masturbation, fellatio, penetration or sodomy," Montréal's strip clubs are *très populaire. Voulez-vous visiter le Club Super Sexe?* (supersexe.ca).

New Orleans

If it's Mardi-Gras, then rent your own balcony (bourbonstreetbalcony.com) overlooking the French Quarter and be prepared to show your stuff and throw some beads. While cruising the bars, take in some zydeco, Cajun and blues, and keep up your strength with large doses of gumbo and jambalaya.

Prague

Often thought of as "the old Krakow," this is practically where beer was invented . . . well, they have a lot of different and exciting varieties, anyway. And then there are the fries—yes, there are 200 strip clubs in town too—but *frites* are the national snack of Belgium, and there's good reason for that. They're great for hangovers . . . and tasty, too.

Reno

Not nearly as wild and hip-hoppin' as Las Vegas, "The Biggest Little City in the World" does—besides gambling and show girls—have many attractions. There is Hot Reno Nights (the classic car show), Street Vibrations (a motorcycle festival) and something called the National Bowling Stadium, dedicated to the sport of bowling. Unfortunately, only tournament players get to bowl in the "Taj Mahal of Tenpins," but you can grab a hot dog and beer and watch!

Riga

Who knew that medieval architecture and bobsledding could go so well together? This Gothic town has lots of bars and strippers but how cool is this—you can bobsled with a member of the Latvian Olympic bobsled team in nearby Sigulda! It beats visiting the gulag at the Occupation Museum (occupationmuseum.lv).

Scottsdale, AZ

One word—golf—and over 200 places to hit the ball around. Oh yeah, and luxury resorts. Nope, this is not a down-and-dirty dive-bar-hopping-vomit-and-strippers kind of place. The wildlife here is found in the surrounding desert. When you're done golfing learn desert survival techniques, gaze up at the brilliant stars through amazingly clear skies or have a cowboy cookout (scottsdale.com).

South Africa
It's a long, long way to go just to get cheap beer. So better to enjoy their fine wines, spend time visiting Robben Island (Nelson Mandela's former prison), go on safari (ccafrica. com) in search of the "Big Five" (lion, leopard, elephant, buffalo, rhino) and cheer for your favorite team in the 2010 World Cup (fifa.com).

South Beach
Beach blankets and bikinis by day, sizzling hotspots by night. This town, a favorite destination for fashion and movie shoots, is known for its model citizenry (literally, they are models) surrounded by lots of Art Deco. Take your place in the middle of it all at the Shore Club (shoreclub.com). And don't forget your skateboard or Rollerblades.

Tijuana
Pass the largest border crossing in the world into a no-frills—but plenty of thrills—party zone. For truly unique entertainment, ask your cab driver about seeing a Tijuana donkey show. And don't forget to pick up some Chiclets on the way home.

Toronto
Like Montréal and all of Canada, there are very liberal laws that barely regulate the interaction between exotic dancer and client. So, though the "loonie" may be catching up to the U.S. dollar, there are still some advantages to heading north if planning a bachelor bacchanal.

Whistler, B.C.
With snowboarding, skiing, hottubbing—even nighttime snowmobiling—Whistler definitely caters to the outdoorsy partier. There are plenty of nightclubs for those who can stay up, and in 2010, spectators too can partake when the Olympics come to town . . . woo hoo Super G!

Slightly Naughty

JOKES!

The centurion was off to the wars to fight Hannibal, and, before taking his leave, he handed over the keys to his house to his closest and most trusted friend, saying, "This is the key to my beautiful wife's chastity girdle. If I should fail to return from the wars in six months, use it. You see, dear friend, to you I entrust everything."

However, the centurion had barely ridden five miles on his way to battle when his trusted friend overtook him, riding at a gallop, and cried, "Dear friend, you gave me the wrong key!"

Bertha was a pert, comely minx who earned her salary working as upstairs maid for wealthy Mrs. Richwitch. However, Bertha was hardly a model of good-nature and, irritated by her continued insolence and inefficiency, Mrs. Richwitch fired her. On receiving her notice, Bertha was frothing mad and lashed out with, "The only reason you're firing me is because you can't stand having a woman better-looking than you around the house. What's more, it was your husband who told me so."

When the horrified Mrs. Richwitch refused to answer her tirade, Bertha blasted on with, "What's more, my figure is sexier than yours . . . and your husband told me that, too!" Then, finally, when Mrs. Richwitch still did not answer, Bertha fired this Parthian shot, "What's more, I'm a lot better in bed than you are, too."

The stunned lady of the house, recovering her powers of speech, gasped, "Did my husband tell you that, too?"

"No, ma'am," Bertha replied. "It was the chauffeur!"

"NOW WATCH THE PRETTY BIRDIE"

DARLING! CAN'T YOU WAIT TILL WE'RE IN THE CABIN?

Hollywood: that's a place where you can pick an orange off a tree and a tomato off any street.

Chaperone: that's a dame who never could make the team but is still in there intercepting passes.

Engagement: a period of urge on the verge of a merge.

Conscience: something that hurts just when everything else feels so good!

Private Ivan Ivanovitch rejoined his Russian infantry battalion in Siberia after a two-weeks leave in Vladivostok. Said a comrade, "What was the first thing you did when you saw Petrushka again?"

"I won't tell you that," replied Ivan, "but I will tell you the second thing I did."

"What was that?" his comrade inquired.

"I took off my skis," said Ivan.

Cohen and Teplitzky went into business manufacturing contraceptives. "You know, Tep," lamented Cohen, "if we were only allowed to advertise our products, we could make ourselves a real bag of dough."

"Right," said Teplitzky, "but how is it possible? They got laws about advertising what we sell."

"Let's go to an agency," said Cohen. "Maybe the gray-flannel-suit guys can come up with a solution."

The partners visited a number of advertising agencies, but were rudely shown the door in every case. Finally, back at their office, Cohen said, "By heaven, we're not licked yet. If those agency creeps won't deal with us, I'll do the job myself. Come in tomorrow, Tep, and I'll have us an ad clean enough to run in a church periodical."

"Oh yeah?" said the more cynical Teplitzky. "The smartest advertising brains in the country won't touch it, but you have the answer."

However, when he came in the next morning, there was Cohen's ad. It read . . .

If you want children,
That's your business.
If you don't
That's ours!

Bachelors know more about women than married men; if they didn't, they'd be married too.

—H. L. Mencken

Fight the Urge

When the groom wakes up "the morning after," hung over and remorseful, he is likely to have this overwhelming urge to confess to his prospective bride all the outrages of the night before. He has to fight this urge. Fighting this and other urges becomes a lifetime activity for many grooms.

—from *Great Bachelor Parties*
by Herb Kavet

Morning-After REMEDIES!

5 TO STAY ALIVE

1 WATER, WAITER. Your body might have been 90 percent water before you went out, but it feels like 20 percent now. Get your dried-up-prune body over to the tap and drink, drink, drink. Drink till your stomach's so full it hurts, then wait. Five minutes later your mouth will be parched and ready for more. Two minutes if you have been smoking.

2 GO BACK TO BED You drank hard, you deserve a good rest. Especially good if you can find someone to wait on your every need.

3 DRINK A SPORTS DRINK You know, like Gatorade or Powerade. You peed out all your body salts, so you'll be needing some more.

4 GET A SUGAR HIT Your body needs sugar to break down alcohol, which means right now it hasn't got any. Which is why you're feeling weak and lightheaded. Mars Bars are good—they only take 15 minutes to start giving you a sugar hit. Jellybeans will really get you bouncing—and they won't make you as fat.

5 PLAY IN THE HAY When you've tried all else (better still, before) settle down to a good old-fashioned romp. The exercise pumps your blood. The rest, well, you know what that does. And at the end you can down a big drink of water and slip back into a peaceful slumber. Ahhh . . .

—The top five "classic" remedies from hungover.net drinkers, er. . . readers.

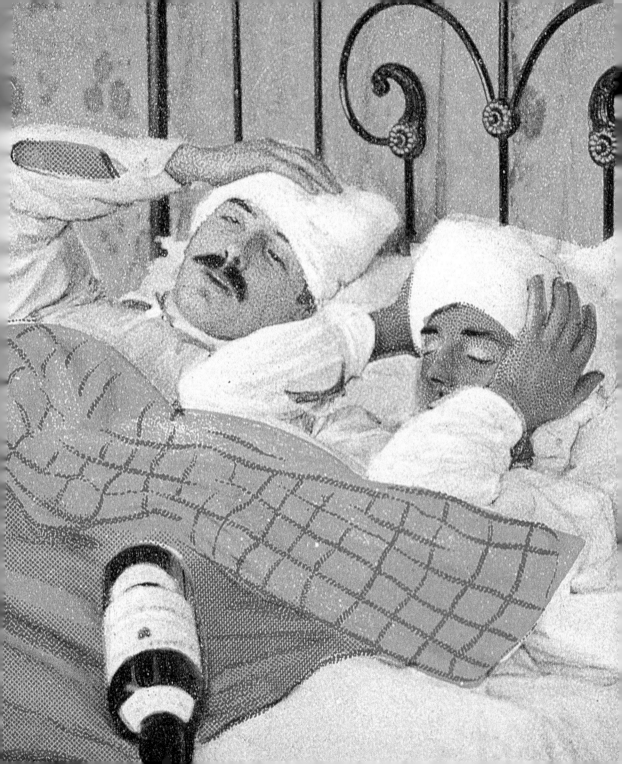

HEALTHY

RICE & BEANS

Rice, grains, cereals, peas and nuts are loaded with Vitamin B1, or Thiamine, which helps metabolize the grog *and* stabilize the nervous system. Lack of B1 is often what causes the infamous DTs, or *delirium tremens*.

TAKE YOUR VITAMINS

Specifically Vitamin B1. B2 is okay, but B1 is the best. To work, however, this cure must be taken *before* you go out and guzzle down that beer. It will make a keg load of difference in the morning.

I COULDA HAD A . . .

One drop of V8 is said by legend to contain an entire bowl of vegetables. Concocted from the mother of all hangover cures—tomato juice—sprinkled with every veggie known to humankind. It couldn't hurt . . . as long as you can keep it down.

KUDZU

Not strictly healthy but close to nature, Kudzu is an Asian vine that has been used for curing hangovers since at least 200 B.C. In 400 A.D. it was written into the Chinese pharmacopeias as a kick-ass cure, and today it's being studied by the Harvard Medical School, which is puzzled by its curative powers.

FREAKISH

HELP THE MEDICINE GO DOWN

In 19th-century England, chimney sweeps swore by the healing properties of a long, warm, soot milkshake. Chim chim cher-ee!

YOU DO THAT VOODOO

According to Haitian voodooists, sticking thirteen black pins in the cork of the offending bottle is well worth a try. This is much more difficult with twist tops—impossible, perhaps, if the hangover is severe.

HARE OF THE . . . (or HARE DOO)

Apparently, in the Wild Wild West, whisky-swilling cowboys swore by a stiff cup of rabbit-droppings tea.

GRAB A NIPPLE

One contributor to an online chatroom swore that "a friend" said that drinking his wife's breast milk cured his hangovers. He tried cow's milk after she stopped lactating, but it didn't work.

ASSYRIAN PASTE

South Africans are said to eat "Assyrian paste": Mix 1 teaspoon of ground swallow's beak with one teaspoon of myrrh. Makes one serving. Helpful hint: eat as quickly as possible and wash down with a glass of water.

HERE'S LOOKIN' AT YOU

When in Outer Mongolia . . . slurp down one pickled sheep's eye in a tall glass of tomato juice.

Obfuscation

What To Do if the Bride Finds Out

Few prospective brides will deny you a little toot, and only a few will complain about a peep show. It's when you touch a tiny bit and maybe get touched back a little that they start to get upset. Here's how to handle it.

1. Deny everything.

2. Claim you were drunk (as likely a state as you can imagine) and you don't remember. (Beware, however, she may not rest until she finds out.)

3. Say the details sound foggily familiar but you think it happened to the best man.

4. Actually, pawning off all despicable acts on the best man is a very sound idea.

GOOD THINGS TO SAY

"God, I just thought about you all evening."

"Oh I had a few drinks and went to bed early."

"The guys wanted to go to a strip place but I find those things so demeaning to women so I went home."

"Harry (*name the best man*) threw up so we went to this car wash to clean up."

"After paintball we had a great time at the arcade and I got the high score on Frogger."

BAD THINGS TO SAY

"You should have seen the size of those bazoongas."

"Can you get STD if you wash right afterwards?"

"I got this funny purple thing on my wee wee."

"The party kind of died when we ran out of condoms."

—from *Great Bachelor Parties* by Herb Kavet

CREDITS

TEXT *Page 14:* From *Adam* magazine. Copyright © 1957 Knight Publishing Corp.; *25:* Excerpted from *Dirty Movies: An Illustrated History of the Stag Film.* Copyright © 1976 by Chelsea House Publishers, an imprint of Infobase Publishing. Reprinted with permission of the publisher.; *47: The Bachelor Party* by Paddy Chayefsky, Copyright © 1955 by Paddy Chayefsky; *55:* From *Great Bachelor Parties* by Herbert I. Kavet © 1998 by Boston America Corp.; *65:* From *Old Mr. Boston DeLuxe Official Bartender's Guide*, Compiled and Edited by Leo Cotton © 1965 Mr. Boston Distiller Inc. Boston, Mass.; *73:* From *Great Bachelor Parties* by Herbert I. Kavet © 1998 by Boston America Corp.; *78:* From *Adam* magazine. Copyright © 1962 Knight Publishing Corp.; *80: Cup Cakes* by Terri "Cup Cake" O'Mason © 1960, FAX Record Company; *86:* "The Girls of Greenwich Village" from *Man's Illustrated* magazine © 1958 by Hanro Corp.; *97: Have a Good Time* by Terri "Cup Cake" O'Mason © 1960, FAX Record Company; *103:* Ultimate Macaroni & Cheese by Cynthia Nims © 2008 MSNBC Interactive; *132–3:* From *Adam* magazine. Copyright © 1958, 1962 Knight Publishing Corp.; *141:* From *Great Bachelor Parties* by Herbert I. Kavet © 1998 by Boston America Corp.; *143:* "Man-Hungry Amazons of Tabasco" from *Man's Illustrated* magazine © 1958 by Hanro Corp.; *156:* "Mating Call" from *Adam* magazine. Copyright © 1957 Knight Publishing Corp.; *164–5:* From *Adam* magazine. Copyright © 1958, 1962 Knight Publishing Corp.; *169:* From *Great Bachelor Parties* by Herbert I. Kavet © 1998 by Boston America Corp.; *174:* From *Great Bachelor Parties* by Herbert I. Kavet © 1998 by Boston America Corp.

IMAGES *Cover & Page 3:* First published 1955. All rights reserved, George Newnes Ltd.; *5:* © 1960 by FAX Record Company; *8:* © BigStockPhoto.com; *37:* Cartoon by Peter Probyn. First published 1955. All rights reserved, George Newnes Ltd.; *39:* Cartoon by A. F. Wiles First published 1955. All rights reserved, George Newnes Ltd.; *57:* © BigStockPhoto.com; *64:* Illustration by Eldon Dedini courtesy of Guilio Dedini; *65:* © BigStockPhoto.com; *67:* Cocktail Napkin by Lenys du Perault; *68:* BACHELOR PARTY © 1984 Twentieth Century Fox. All rights reserved.; *71:* MEXICAN SUNRISE © 2008 Red J Films. All rights reserved. Written and directed by Rowdy Stovall; *72:* Copyright 1953 Reamer Keller and Percy Barker; *76:* From *Adam* magazine. Copyright © 1957 Knight Publishing Corp.; *77:* © BigStockPhoto.com; *78:* Illustration by Bill Edwards, *Adam* magazine. Copyright © 1962 Knight Publishing Corp.; *81:* Record cover from Dooto Records; *85:* Cocktail Napkin design by Zinna; *87:* Illustration from *French Frills* magazine, © American Art Agency, Inc. 1961; *95:* Cocktail Napkin design by Zinna; *96: Spice After Hours* record cover illustration © 1962, FAX Record Company; *98:* Illustration by W. W. Denslow from *The Wonderful Wizard of Oz* by L. Frank Baum; *99:* Image courtesy of Rob Dawson at SoVeryWrong.com; *111:* Shakespeare "Howls" Cocktail Napkin; *113: Saturday Nite Riot* © 1960 by FAX Record Company; *114: Safe Sex no. 1* © Heere Heeresma Jr. 1984; *115:* Adult Super Sperm Costume courtesy of FindCostume.com; *116:* Peepshow Shot Glasses designed by Anouk Jansen (Jansen+co) for Fred, FredAndFriends.com; *117:* ButtHead! photo courtesy of PerpetualKid.com, Beer Belt image courtesy of BaronBob.com, possibly the world's wackiest gift gallery!; *120:* Fighter pilot image courtesy of Flightdeck Air Combat Center at FlightDeck1.com; *121:* Cigar photo courtesy of Excitations.com, Lost In Space® B-9™ Robot image courtesy of Hammacher Schlemmer, Gag Cockroaches image courtesy X-treme Geek © E-filliate Corporation; *123:* Shakespeare "Howls" Cocktail Napkin; *124–7:* T-shirt designs © 2009 Night & Day Design, LLC; *125, 126, 129:* © BigStockPhoto.com; *130–1:* © 2006 Zorb® Ltd.; *135, 138:* © BigStockPhoto.com; *140:* © 1953 Reamer Keller and Percy Barker; *142–9:* from *Man's Illustrated* magazine © 1958 by Hanro Corp.; *155:* © BigStock Photo.com; *156:* "Mating Call" from *Adam* magazine. Copyright © 1957 Knight Publishing Corp.

Every effort has been made to contact all copyright holders; any errors or omissions are inadvertent and will be corrected upon notice in future reprintings.